Africa's Stalled Development

AFRICA'S STALLED DEVELOPMENT

International Causes and Cures

David K. Leonard
Scott Straus

LYNNE
RIENNER
PUBLISHERS

BOULDER
LONDON

Published in the United States of America in 2003 by
Lynne Rienner Publishers, Inc.
1800 30th Street, Boulder, Colorado 80301
www.rienner.com

and in the United Kingdom by
Lynne Rienner Publishers, Inc.
3 Henrietta Street, Covent Garden, London WC2E 8LU

Library of Congress Cataloging-in-Publication Data
Leonard, David K.
  Africa's stalled development : international causes and cures / David K. Leonard and
Scott Straus.
     p.   cm.
  Includes bibliographical references and index.
  ISBN 978-1-58826-140-3 (alk. paper)
  ISBN 978-1-58826-116-8 (pbk. : alk. paper)
     1. Africa—Economic conditions—1960–   2. Africa—Economic policy.
3. Africa—Politics and government—1960–   4. Debts, External—Africa.
5. Technical assistance—Africa.   I. Straus, Scott, 1970–   II. Title.

HC800.L465 2003
338.967—dc21
                                                                                    2002031839

British Cataloguing in Publication Data
A Cataloguing in Publication record for this book
is available from the British Library.

Printed and bound in the United States of America

   The paper used in this publication meets the requirements
       of the American National Standard for Permanence of
       Paper for Printed Library Materials Z39.48-1992.

     10   9   8   7   6   5   4

Contents

Tables

Preface

Joseph Conrad's century-old image of the "heart of darkness" has stuck to sub-Saharan Africa with depressing if mistaken persistence.[1] The rest of the world sees Africa as the locus of civil war, ethnic strife, autocracy, economic stagnation, and the plagues of AIDS and malaria. This dark image is grossly exaggerated. The majority of the countries of Africa are at peace; ethnic cooperation is far more prevalent than conflict; democracy is prospering in Botswana, Ghana, and Senegal and is promising for South Africa and Nigeria; strong economic growth is evident in Botswana, Ghana, Tanzania, and Uganda; and the incidence of AIDS declines markedly as one moves west from central Africa. Thus the picture for Africa south of the Sahara desert is brighter than the world believes.

But that is not to say that it is good. Even if Rwanda has been the sole site of genocide on the continent in the forty years since independence in the 1960s, that is one incidence too many; economic growth in sub-Saharan Africa is lackluster; authoritarian regimes are the rule; the impacts of AIDS and malaria are devastating; and one-quarter of the region's fifty-four countries are or have recently been at war, usually a civil one.[2]

Poverty, autocracy, disease, war—something can be said about each of these dreadful horsemen of the apocalypse. But most problems on the continent derive from the nature of Africa's relationship to the international system and the weak states it has fostered there.[3] International trade and development assistance in their present forms have produced scant development; technical assistance has left local organizational capacity seriously deficient; and humanitarian military intervention has failed to bring peace or protect basic human rights. The continent's current interactions with the international system create a deeply dysfunctional set of incentives for development, democracy, and civil order. Only if these relationships are restructured and positive incentives created is the region likely to escape its present trap of underdevelopment. In this way, Africa can regain the ability to be the agent, rather than the victim, of its own destiny.

In this book, we seek to elucidate and advocate for those functional incentives. In doing so, we are deliberately trying to think "outside the box" of conventional alternatives—for they are not working. The empirical regularities we find in African politics and economics are not new; we are building on the exciting work of many other contemporary scholars. The difference lies in the way these regularities are pulled together and the policy conclusions drawn from them. Perhaps others will find flaws in the analysis and offer still other policy choices. But if in doing so they too take the discussion onto new ground, we will have met our objectives of stimulating fresh thinking about Africa's contemporary crisis.

In the first chapter, we explore the nature of African political systems, which the label "personal rule" captures well. While endorsing this general view of African politics, we argue that the foundations of personal rule remain poorly understood. We propose that the structure of colonial states, an international system that rewards statehood in name but not in practice, and postindependence Africa's narrow economic base are the foundations for weak states and personal rule in Africa. We contend that dysfunctions are particularly likely to emerge when African economies are dominated by the production of primary product exports—especially natural resources—from geographically isolated areas ("enclaves").

The heavy burden of international debt on Africa is examined in Chapter 2, together with the extreme dependence on overseas aid that has followed from it. The result is that African elites—political, economic, and social—are externally oriented and insufficiently focused on the domestic opportunities that would produce sustainable development. We advocate the cancellation of all debt and the reduction of aid in order to return the initiative for Africa's development to Africans themselves.

Technical assistance is the subject of Chapter 3. It has produced a dualistic market for expertise and managerial skill, vastly increasing costs and making locals much less likely to fill these posts. We argue that greatly reduced technical assistance could be used to restructure local career systems and create significantly improved incentives for indigenous managers.

In Chapter 4, we return to the consequences of economic dependence on the export of primary products created in enclaves. We demonstrate that the ease with which such income streams can be controlled and "taxed" by small military forces makes them a fertile breeding ground for civil conflict in the context of weak states.

Given the foregoing, Africa will need external assistance if it is to break the vicious circle of violence and state decline in which it is currently caught. In Chapter 5, we present a proposal for the international military guarantee of the continent's democracies against coups and rebellions—so that when members of African states have gained the right to govern their own destiny, it is protected from the soldiers and dictators who would take it from them.

This book grows out of the nearly forty years David Leonard has devoted to problems of African development and the half-dozen years Scott Straus has spent as a journalist covering east and central Africa and as a doctoral student. The specific impetus for the book came from an invitation from Haverford College to David Leonard to lecture on these themes in March 2001.

We would like to acknowledge the comments and assistance provided by Vinod Aggarwal, Sam Angus, Kathy Barnart, Mara Cheng, Sophal Ear, James Fearon, Dennis Galvan, Donald Groom, Goran Hyden, Thorsten Janus, Peter Lewis, John McCarthy, Rwekaza Mukandala, Mugumo Mushi, Carl Pennypacker, Richard Roberts, Donald Rothchild, Fred Schaeffer, Gail Stern, Richard Tittle, and Steve Weber. We are grateful. Scott Straus's research for the book was supported with a National Science Foundation Graduate Research Fellowship.

—*David K. Leonard*
—*Scott Straus*

1

The Contemporary African State: The Politics of Distorted Incentives

SUB-SAHARAN AFRICA'S DEVELOPMENT PROBLEMS ARE INSEPARABLE FROM its politics. International economic forces well beyond sub-Saharan Africa's control have hobbled the continent, but some countries have been able to adopt public policies that have improved their development performance.[1] Why have only relatively few countries in Africa succeeded in making the changes necessary to improve their economic performance since the 1960s? The short answer is that the dynamics of African politics have worked against policies that would lead to greater development.

In this chapter, we first describe the political dynamics that characterize sub-Saharan African politics. We call them the "personal rule paradigm," thus drawing on a concept that captures the continent's modal form of politics. However, although this framework is powerful in descriptive terms, it is less adept at explaining where the dynamics it describes come from and how they are sustained over the long term. The remainder of the chapter is devoted to elucidating the underlying institutions and structures—and their international connections—that allow "personal rule" to persist on the continent. If sub-Saharan Africa is to improve its developmental prospects, we need to understand these institutions and structures and their international connections.

The Personal Rule Paradigm

The standard popular image of Africa is a continent of corrupt dictators who preside over fractious populations. The cliché used to describe this is "Big Man" politics.[2] Even if this image is catchy and is what academics call "journalistic," this understanding of African politics has a long pedigree in scholarship on the continent. Indeed, it reflects an academic consensus about the modal dynamics of African politics—the personal rule paradigm.

In the context of African politics, Robert Jackson and Carl Rosberg popularized the term "personal rule" in an influential book by that name in the early 1980s.[3] However, before and since then, scholars have used other terms—"patrimonialism," "neopatrimonialism," "prebendalism," and "sultanism"—that essentially capture, with small but important differences between them, the main dynamics connoted by personal rule. A number of recent influential studies effectively agree that a version of personal rule is the main form of politics in Africa.[4] Although to the lay reader these concepts may seem archaic, taken together they go a long way in explaining African politics and the continent's development problems.

As with many key social science terms, personal rule can be traced back to Max Weber, for whom patrimonialism was an instance of "traditional authority."[5] Weber defined a political system as patrimonial when its administrative and military staff were considered the personal retainers of the head of state.[6] The key characteristics of these systems are that (1) appointment and position generally depend on loyalty to one's superior and not on adherence to impersonal norms, (2) transactions are personalized and office is treated as a form of personal property and a source of private gain (which Weber called a prebend), and (3) a clear sense of a public interest that transcends private ones does *not* exist.[7]

In the African context, personal rule is often shorthand for describing the prevalence of patronage politics: the distribution of public goods—offices, public works projects, permits, tax breaks, and so on—in return for loyalty. Used in this way, the state operates less according to procedural rules and more by personal relationships. "Clientelism" is another term for this dynamic. Personal, informal dynamics here are of foremost importance, not abstract bureaucratic laws.

Of course, corruption is related to patronage politics. A key feature of patrimonialism is that a public office is treated as personal property.

In such a case, a public office becomes a means for extracting private wealth, which is essentially another way of describing corruption. Stealing money is probably not the common form of corruption in a personal rule system, even though that may be the first image that leaps to mind. Rather, corruption more frequently takes the form of using public office with the intention of building private power and accumulating private capital, whether through business deals, property purchases, concessionary taxes, or other means of manipulating public office for personal gain.

Since the early 1980s, researchers have widely endorsed this vision of African politics. Jackson and Rosberg's influential study highlighted what they believed to be the most important elements of a patrimonial system—namely, politics in which African heads of state play a pivotal, overbearing, and often Machiavellian role.[8] Jean-Francois Médard, as well as Michael Bratton and Nicolas van de Walle, employ the term "neopatrimonialism" to stress that personal rule dynamics operate within modern bureaucracies. Neopatrimonial politics are not "traditional" as Weber first conceptualized them, they argue, but a contemporary and sophisticated adaptation.[9] Both points are correct, we believe. To stress the overlap in all these analyses and to employ a more accessible term, we have chosen the "personal rule system" for all these insights. However, in choosing personal rule to label the characteristics of Africa's predominant political system, the point is not to emphasize the personalities of individual leaders. Rather, the point is to stress the notion of a system—an interlinked set of norms and practices—that is reproduced irrespective of the attributes of a given head of state.

That said, a personal rule system is one in which politics are eminently presidential. Little distinction is made between the ruler and the state—an extreme form of seeing government as personal property— and the ruler's personal decisions always take precedence over formal laws. Here again, public life revolves around the president; power is personalized; it is the private affair of the leader. Politics are not beholden to formal procedures but to personal decisions.

This summary is not meant to be exhaustive but rather to provide an overview of the key features of most African polities: patronage, clientelism, corruption, presidentialism, informalism, and personalized relationships. Some of these terms may be cumbersome, but bearing them in mind provides a complex picture of the central dynamics in most contemporary African political systems. These features are particularly important for their consequences.

The key consequence is that personal rule contributes to weak states.[10] Procedures based on loyalty, informal agreements, and personal relationships tend to undermine a government's ability to function effectively. Of course, no system is purely based on formal or informal procedures. But in a personal rule system, informal procedures trump formal ones, including those that might outlast their leaders, which has the effect of undermining forms of capable administration.

Similarly, in a personal rule system, public resources tend to be used for patronage or private purposes, resulting in a lack of public investment. Governments do not plan for a common good; they purvey private accumulation. This can be true even at the most banal level of maintaining road networks, but is even more apparent in the lack of long-range planning needed for development. Another way of making this point is to recall that "the public" is not an effective idea in a personal rule system.[11] The state is not a tool for public development but for private "eating" and for rewarding support networks.[12] In the extreme, this dynamic can hollow out states. After years of private pocketing of public wealth, distribution of largesse to clients, scant investment in public administration, and factional intrigue, very little is left. Gutted and neglected, over time states can collapse.[13]

The politics of personal rule also tend to revolve less around ideological positions and more around factions. Why? The key quality to possess in a personal rule system is loyalty to a superior, and the most effective position is to be in favor with the president. Thus in a personal rule system, rather than staking out policy positions, elites in and around government tend to jockey for position in order to gain access to the president, often with the intent of demonstrating their loyalty. An adept personal ruler rotates his favor, never letting any one potential rival gain too much power. Politics are not fought over who is left, liberal, or right, but over who can be trusted. Politics of trust and loyalty easily spill over into ethnic politics. As a presumed community of kin, a ruler's most loyal supporters are seen to be his or her ethnic group.

These characterizations may sometimes be exaggerated, and they are not as universally present as is sometimes implied. There are positive counterexamples, but they are exceptions.[14] The broad picture conforms far too often to these various images from the literature.

On the economic terrain, personal rule has been used to explain much of Africa's lackluster performance. A basic insight of students of late developing economies is that effective bureaucracies and government investment in infrastructure are the sine qua non for economic growth. Personal rule thus undermines the very institutions that would facilitate development.[15] Economists also have pinpointed reliable domestic policy as a key factor for economic growth.[16] Personal rule is the antithesis of predictable policy: the demands of survival and the realities of personal rule dictate rapidly changing, unforeseeable government measures. This lack of predictability is inimical to the "calculability nexus" that most argue is essential for capitalist development.[17] Unpredictable policy, weak infrastructure, high inflation, and taxes based more on distributional and loyalty concerns add up to high costs of doing business for both local and international investors.[18] Over time, patronage politics create an inflationary spiral of state expenditures, all too often leading to ultimate fiscal collapse.

Problems with the Personal Rule Framework

The concept of personal rule provides a powerful analytic framework for understanding Africa's problems with development. The short synopsis presented here is testament to the range of phenomena the framework explains. Virtually no student of African politics denies the prevalence of these phenomena; indeed, that is why personal rule (neopatrimonialism) has become the standard basis for understanding African politics. But the framework is not without problems.

A common critique is that patronage, clientelism, and corruption are prevalent in many places, including many comparatively wealthy and developed Western countries. Italy is the most-cited example. In the United States, the names electorates and scholars pin on patronage politics are "pork barrel" and "machine" politics. But almost everywhere, governments survive and gain support through distributing goods and services. An Africanist, of course, would counter that the problem on the continent is the overwhelming predominance of personal rule politics to the virtual exclusion of other state practices.

We would point to a more fundamental problem with the personal rule framework: that the concept serves as both cause and consequence. Indeed, if Africanists agree on the prevalence and effects of personal rule dynamics, few focus on where the phenomenon comes from in the first place. As a result, the causes of personal rule and the reasons for its prevalence on the continent remain poorly understood.

Still, a few plausible explanations are embedded in different analyses. One school of thought on personal rule emphasizes that the phenomenon is rooted in the "economy of affection" of peasant society.[19] In subsistence economies, human relationships and personal social exchange networks ensure individual security against disease, disability, old age, and misfortune. Insurance is not based on impersonal rights or formal institutions but on kinship, friendship, and dependence on the advantaged. These social systems lead easily and naturally into patron-client relationships, and it therefore was easy and natural in the past to build patronage systems on their foundations. However, this "traditional" root to personal rule has rapidly diminishing importance today as the gap between elites and masses in Africa has widened and the former show much less obligation toward and dependence on the latter.

A second, related argument is that personal rule is cultural. The central point here is that its dynamics derive from deeply embedded norms in society, whether peasant or not. African rulers thus distribute resources because popular support for their rule depends on it.[20] Fine-grained studies of what "democracy" means to African electorates lend credence to this claim.[21] Similarly, the politics of personal rule can be thought to grow out of ethnicity's salience in Africa. If ethnic ties and ethnic worldviews are seen as dominant in Africa, the argument goes, they would dictate personal rule politics where presumed kin ties trump other bases of interaction.

A third plausible explanation claims that personal rule stems from the existence of multinational states in Africa. This argument points to the fact that the continent's states are legacies of artificial colonial entities that grouped together disparate communities. Centrifugal forces thus bedevil the postcolonial state, with various ethnic groups constantly opting out of national cooperation. Patronage politics are a way of holding people together across ethnic and religious divides when they have little loyalty to the state itself. The problem here is that personal rule politics are present as well in monoethnic states, such as Somalia, and do not correlate with numbers of ethnic groups. Zimbabwe, with relatively few ethnic groups, seems as given to personal rule as Tanzania, with more than 100.

A fourth possible cause of personal rule is the weakness of African states. Presidentialism is a response to lack of effective formal institutions; patronage is a way of gaining compliance in the context of little legitimacy and weak coercive capacity. This latter point is rooted in colonialism. Lacking legitimacy with its subjects, the colonial state used a combination of ruthless coercion and material benefits to create and sustain local patrons, who in turn controlled their populations. The postcolonial state has less ability to coerce its subjects, leading to a heavier reliance on patronage.

Although each of these approaches offers insight into the roots of the politics of personal rule, none offers a clear causal path or explains its persistence in the present. Analyses that hinge on personal rule often stall in explanatory cul-de-sacs. Take the crucial example of weak states. On the one hand, personal rule is seen to cause weak states: patronage, corruption, and personalism all undermine the development of capable public administration and gnaw away at state legitimacy. On the other hand, personal rule is seen as the consequence of weak states: patronage, corruption, and personalism all are responses to weak formal institutions. Lacking legitimacy and strong national communities, patronage is the path to political elites' survival. Personal rule is thus both cause and effect of Africa's weak states.

Similarly, ethnicity serves as both the source and consequence of personal rule. In such a system, loyalty, personal networks, and trust matter most; this situation creates politicized ethnic ties. But ethnicity also leads to personal rule in the sense that strong communal bonds encourage loyalty and personal ties as well as use of the state to distribute rewards to a leader's ethnic group. Which comes first—ethnicity or personal rule? That question is impossible to answer. A similar problem confronts cultural explanations of personal rule. Did a mode of personal rule create a norm of personal rule politics, or did the norm create the mode?

From a theoretical point of view, the disadvantages of causal circularity are clear. Certainly it is possible for social phenomena to reinforce each other and thus act as both cause and effect. But there needs to be a starting point. Causal circularity has practical problems too: without clearly identifying the causal source, restorative action has no place to start. For these reasons and based on our empirical analysis, we have looked elsewhere for the cause and sustaining force behind personal rule.

In our search for causes, we therefore stress the historical and political economy roots of personal rule, especially the prevalence of what we will call "enclave economies" on the continent. These factors, we claim, are important among the causes of Africa's personal rule politics but even more central in their continuation. The analysis is not meant to exclude cultural or ethnic factors or dismiss the possibility that patronage is a rational response to fractious, diverse populations. Rather, the point is to emphasize the primacy of historical and political economy reasons for the prevalence *and sustenance* of personal rule in Africa. This analysis can also explain the prevalence of civil conflict on the continent.

Weak States and the International System

Empirically, weak states characterize and distinguish sub-Saharan Africa, with the exception of South Africa.[22] Africa's relationship with the world outside the continent, in particular the West, has produced and still is producing weak states. The key external legacy that ultimately resulted in weak states in Africa is colonialism, which built on a weakened and fractured political landscape left behind after decades of the transcontinental slave trade. With the exception of Ethiopia, African states today derive from the institutional legacies of nineteenth- and twentieth-century European colonial rule.[23]

It is plausible that the slave trade also contributed to a legacy of weak states in Africa. However, this assertion is the subject of much debate among historians of precolonial Africa. As nonhistorians, we believe the transcontinental slave trade had the effect of encouraging compact, raiding political units and rendering larger states less attractive. African political elites who built strong militaries during the period of the transatlantic slave trade could gain much more from raiding and selling the labor power of their neighbors than they could from incorporating those families into their territories and taxing their production. In our estimation, the loss of many productive members of society, the destructive penetration of the African hinterland, and the political conflicts that the slave trade inspired or intensified had a significant negative impact on the continent's state development. In a period when other states were consolidating control and laying important institutional foundations for state building, African political systems were seeing their scarcest productive resource (labor) skimmed off in a highly exploitative industry. When observing time periods of up to fifty years in Africa, one may see strengthened state power in regional contexts, as one military power emerged temporarily hegemonic. But over the long term, the patterns of investment in the means of destruction (Jack Goody's term), as opposed to the means of production, had deep and lasting negative consequences, as did the exchange of captives for consumer goods. We recognize that the slave trade did contribute to the formation of kingdoms, that the trade's intensity and impact varied across the continent, and that slaving had existed in many African countries prior to the transcontinental forms across the Atlantic and Indian oceans. But the magnitude of the transcontinental trade, in particular across the Atlantic Ocean, had qualitatively different effects and the states that emerged all too often depended on the export rather than the use of labor. Thus we side with those historians who believe the slave trade inhibited state growth in Africa.[24] Our overall analysis does not depend on this point, however.

Returning then to colonialism as the key causal factor, its character in Africa is the subject of long-standing disagreements among Africanists. Some characterize the colonial state as raw coercive power; Crawford Young's label, *bula matari* (rock crusher), aptly captures this image of the African colonial state.[25] So does Mahmood Mamdani's concept of "decentralized despotism."[26] These scholars trace authoritarianism in contemporary states to colonial institutions. By contrast, other scholars characterize the colonial African state as ineffective, underfunded, constantly negotiating local conditions, and forced into indirect rule. They depict a colonial administration full of internal contradictions and struggling to stay afloat. Sara Berry's evocative expression for the colonial state is thus "hegemony on a shoestring"—although she would not deny its raw coercion.[27]

Both analyses of African colonialism point to the same outcome: weak states. The *bula matari* image captures an important dimension of Africa's colonial experience: namely, that externally sourced coercion guaranteed colonial states. Colonial states were effective enough in projecting power over their territories so that no other legitimate political entities were able to challenge their authority. However, in using the threat of organized force to protect states, colonial authorities worked without popular legitimacy or penetrative administrative institutions. Therein lay a long-standing weakness: African states had precious few domestic sources of strength. Even if colonial authorities offered material advantages to their local collaborators, this largesse was too limited to secure any domestic depth to states.

To the extent colonial states earned sanctioned recognition, legitimacy rested on inter-European understandings. In large measure, states were states because European powers said they were, and each power had an interest in maintaining the existing system. State financing, too, rested on the colonizing power. Though harsh taxes were introduced to finance the apparatus of the colonial government, the threat of European military intervention was necessary to collect them, and state budgets often depended on supplements from Europe. At the end of the day, then, African colonial states depended on external sources for their survival. States survived through a combination of the threat of superior physical force, the strength of inter-European agreements, and European financing that largely built infrastructure and co-opted local powerbrokers. When states faced any real and direct challenge, survival ultimately depended on the willingness of the European colonizer to intervene militarily to sustain it—as it did, for example, in Kenya during the Mau Mau rebellion after World War II.

External sources, however, did not imbue states with rock-crushing power over those citizens beyond their immediate reach. Here the "hegemony on a shoestring" image brings into relief the reality of Africa's colonial experience. The bureaucracies built under colonialism were in most cases far more extensive than preexisting administrative institutions. But their capacity and depth should not be overestimated. Colonialism designed institutions that would primarily benefit Europe or a small settler class. As such, the institutions that developed politically served an urban few and were economically centered on exports.

By the dawn of independence, colonial state institutions had only partially transformed the African landscape. Africa had centralized bureaucracies, nominally modern infrastructure, monetized market economies, a dual system of law, and new cultural systems. States that oversaw these institutions covered newly crafted territories. But overall, the states were not powerful: they were marked by "shoestring" budgets, constant compromise with whichever local actors could be brought online, and external sources of power.[28] In short, even if the colonial states' internal apparatuses were strong, even if they were far more developed than the preexisting institutions, and even if they were authoritarian, their reach and depth were limited. When attempts were made to extend states out from the colonial capital, the states were forced to compromise with local forces on the ground. The net result was that the colonial state system was coercive but not strong.

Africa's transition to self-rule did not substantially alter this picture. Weak states persisted. Statehood continued to derive primarily from the international system: from states in other regions, from bilateral donors in the West and elsewhere, and from international organizations such as the United Nations. In continuing to source statehood externally, political institutions remained weak. Domestic sources of statehood remained secondary, and power continued to be concentrated in the hands of the few. Economies continued to benefit urban areas, and trade remained externally focused.[29] In short, the transfer of sovereignty to African rulers did not change the basis of statehood in Africa.

This vision of postcolonial Africa endorses the long-standing Africanist observation that many of the region's countries possess juridical statehood but lack its empirical attributes.[30] Assuming a Weberian definition of the state, empirical statehood refers to an administrative organization that enjoys a monopoly on the exercise of legitimate force within defined territorial boundaries.[31] A number of African political entities lack control over the legitimate exercise of coercion within their boundaries, but they are nonetheless recognized ("juridically") by the international system as states and derive significant resources from that recognition.[32]

Even if other indicators of empirical statehood are employed—for example, financial self-sufficiency, leadership of national political communities, or performance of basic services such as road maintenance—many African political entities fare poorly. Statehood is not rooted in domestic relations. Rather, in Africa it is sustained by the international system. The continent's states persist as internationally recognized and funded "juridical entities" or as "quasi-states" without sufficient domestic bases of support.[33] This postcolonial dynamic effectively continues patterns of statehood that developed under colonialism.

Foreign aid remittances are a case in point. In the period since independence, African state budgets have become increasingly dependent on aid. Foreign aid accounts for more than half of gross domestic investment in many African countries.[34] The average sub-Saharan African country receives upward of four times more official development assistance as a percentage of gross domestic product (GDP) than states in other world regions.[35] In the 1990s, aid reached an average of $35 per capita in sub-Saharan Africa.[36] In some countries, it sometimes reached staggering levels—for five African states, aid represented at least one-fifth of gross national product (GNP) at some point in the 1990s, and in one year it stood at 42 percent for Mozambique.[37]

If foreign aid is one benefit of "juridical" statehood (i.e., recognition under international law), there are others. William Reno's work on "warlord" states shows how international recognition is an instrument leaders use to secure lucrative commercial contracts with multinational corporations and to gain huge international loans. Warlords, he argues, seek to maximize the benefits of possessing the right to "juridical" sovereignty, but without building their states. Indeed, when facing armed rivals, leaders would rather weaken state institutions—that way, opponents will either have less incentive to capture the center or have weaker institutions if they control peripheries.[38] Not coincidentally, "warlord" commercial deals often revolve around enclave production. In fact, the four countries that Reno profiles—Sierra Leone, Liberia, the Democratic Republic of Congo, and Nigeria—have economies in which mining or estate agriculture production accounts for the overwhelming bulk of state revenue and GDP. It is to this feature—enclave production—that we now turn.

Personal Rule and Enclave Production

The above analysis provides a historical basis for understanding the prevalence of weak states on the continent. Rather than seeing personal rule and weak states as indistinguishable parts of the same package or viewing personal rule as causing weak states, we have argued for a long-range view of why states in Africa tend to have weak institutional capacities: weak states are rooted in the institutions established under colonialism.

However, this argument does not exhaust the explanation of why states remain weak or why patronage and distributional politics are such predominant features of African politics. Nor does it explain why postcolonial states have not mutated into more representative institutions that preside over national political communities. In this section, we root these features of personal rule in the continent's political economy. We argue that enclave production and, to a lesser degree, foreign aid provide structural bases for these other major dynamics of African politics.

Enclave production entails export of primary products (usually extractive) that are generated in a small area. In Africa, the prevalent forms of enclave production are mining, oil drilling, and agricultural production on the estates of large corporations. The enclave idea implies that production is geographically concentrated, that a large portion of the land or capital goods involved in export production cannot easily be assigned to other profitable purposes, and that labor (which always is mobile) is a small part of the cost of production. Most states on the continent have a tax base that is built overwhelmingly on exports, and many derive most of their export income from enclave production, making the latter "enclave economies."[39]

Two other general features of enclave economies should be stressed at the outset: first, that enclave economies are "rentier," and second, that they do not depend on widespread productivity in the population. Regarding the first point, states "tax" enclaves for a firm's right to do business in a particular place, using both official taxes and the collection of bribes. However, the state itself does not contribute significantly to the value of production, sometimes not even through provision of physical infrastructure or assurance of security. In that sense, states collect "rents" from these economic activities: they collect revenue, but they do not add to production.

Regarding the second point, in enclave economies production is disconnected from the overall economic productivity of the general population. Revenue generation is physically confined to small areas, and the main markets are external, thus making the general economic health of areas outside the enclave quite secondary, if not irrelevant. In enclave economies, then, elites gain little from any deep, growing, economic prosperity of the mass of the population.

Mobutu Sese Seko's Democratic Republic of Congo (then called Zaire) was an extreme example of an enclave economy. In his thirty-two years in power, Mobutu succeeded in generating huge amounts of wealth for himself and for his clients, while 99 percent of that country's population—some 39 million people—faced a disintegrating economy. To survive, Mobutu only needed to maintain diamond, gold, copper, cobalt, and other mines as well as collect foreign aid to protect his state and perpetuate his rule.

Senegal is a good counterexample of an economy that does not rely on enclaves. The country's prosperity is highly dependent on the export of cotton and groundnuts, but both of these products are grown over wide areas by smallholders. The welfare of both the state and Senegal's politically important Muslim brotherhoods is therefore dependent on the economic productivity of the mass of the peasantry.[40]

Enclave economies, we argue, are a foundation for personal rule. In such regimes, rather than developing infrastructure or institutional capacities for broad-based markets, states collect and distribute "rents" (taxes and bribes) as patronage. An enclave economic base allows personal rule to sustain itself over the long run both because enclaves themselves are susceptible to state predation and because enclaves do not depend on widespread productivity for their sustenance. Thus, the state's primary function can be private patronage distribution because wealth generation does not depend on development.[41] Combined with (and reinforcing) weak states, this economic base locks African countries into poorly performing political and economic patterns that can lead to bureaucratic and fiscal collapse, as well as to civil conflict. Let us take this argument in parts.

One of the key findings of the cross-national, econometric research of Paul Collier and his associates at the World Bank is a strong correlation between civil conflict and dependence on primary products for export revenues.[42] (Primary products include minerals, other natural resources, and agricultural goods.) J. D. Sachs and M. Werner also find these natural resource–dependent economies have lower rates of economic growth.[43] What is the causal mechanism that would underlie such associations? Collier and his colleagues suggest that this type of production is easily attached by rebel groups to support their military operations and therefore provides incentives to rebellion. We think these findings are immensely important, and they are central to our analysis. Nonetheless, if susceptibility to predation (and more broadly the centrality of "economic rents") is the mechanism both for conflict and low rates of economic growth, we think that the concept "dependence on primary products for export revenues" is too broad a concept to explain Africa's problems and that "enclave production" gets much closer to the causal dynamics at work. Another team at Stanford University, James D. Fearon and David D. Laitin, doubt the Collier group's emphasis on primary product export dependence as a source of civil conflict. However, they *do* find evidence that oil producers may be more susceptible to civil conflict, which fits with our broader thesis that the factor driving civil conflict in Africa is dependence on enclave production (an interpretation to which they explicitly remain open).[44]

"Enclave production" is more precise because not all forms of agricultural production are subject to predation. Labor-intensive annual crops that can be grown over wide areas and do not require complicated, expensive processing—such as cotton, groundnuts, maize (corn), and rice—typically provide modest profits to the grower. These crops are generally produced by smallholders in Africa, and if the state or anyone else tries to extract too great a tax from their export, the peasant growers will simply switch crops or withdraw into subsistence. These products also cannot be moved to ports without fairly great investments by the state in roads. Tree crops, such as coffee, tea, and cocoa, would seem to offer greater predatory opportunities—traditionally they have commanded higher international prices relative to the labor costs involved in their production, and once the investment has been made in bringing the tree to maturity, the producer will continue to find it worthwhile to pick the crop even when prices drop significantly. When the producers are smallholders, however, it turns out that the predatory opportunities have stricter limits than imagined—infrastructural investments have a large effect on the profits to be made from the crops, and the experience of numerous African states indicates that if outside agents extract too high a percentage of the crop's value, peasants simply smuggle the crops to better markets in other states or withdraw into subsistence.[45] It is much easier to prey on estate producers of these tree crops—they are large enough to provide their own infrastructure, and for capitalists, subsistence production is not an option, causing them to produce much longer under conditions of declining profits.

The New Institutional Economists, particularly Oliver Williamson, make the point that the greater the extent to which the value of a particular piece of property is tied to its use for a specific purpose—what they call "asset specificity"—the more the owner loses bargaining power.[46] Tree crops have more asset specificity than annuals. So too do products that can be mined or ones grown or made only in unusual places. These latter products have a higher value, but because the land cannot easily be turned to other profitable purposes, the enterprises lose flexibility. Expensive and complicated processing plants that can be used for only one crop also carry asset specificity with them. All these aspects of dedicated assets create opportunities for predation, for the owners will want to pay off those who threaten production rather than lose their investment by switching to another product or shutting down.[47]

From the preceding two paragraphs, it is evident that items produced in capital-heavy enclaves are more susceptible to predation. That makes them much more attractive targets for both personal rulers and predatory rebels than are smallholder agriculturists because neither predation nor general state or market collapse will stop the revenue from flowing: even if their profits are often looted, enclave producers will continue to generate goods because of extreme asset specificity, and because of regional concentration, production will continue even in the face of general collapse.

Thomas Tomich, Peter Kilby, and Bruce Johnston have advanced a number of economic and welfare arguments for the advantages of more egalitarian, labor-intensive modes of agricultural production, as opposed to large, capital-intensive ones that rely on migratory labor—which they call unimodal versus bimodal systems.[48] We find a state-building argument as well, and one that helps explain the extreme forms of personal rule in some parts of the continent. The large estates of a bimodal system are much more likely to be geographically concentrated and somewhat more capable and willing to sustain production in a hostile state environment. Thus they also tend toward being enclaves.[49] The Firestone rubber estates of Liberia are a good example of export agricultural production that did *not* rely on the state for general economic infrastructure.

One key element of personal rule is counterproductive development policy in the forms of unpredictable economic policy and strategies of private accumulation through public means. Although a personal rule framework alone might stress "culture" as the root of this problem, enclave production better explains the persistence of these policies. Focusing on enclave production does not explain the motives behind such actions—motives that, in any case, are not exceptional or specific to Africa. Rather, the enclave economy framework underlines both the feasibility of this mode and the absence of incentives and institutions that would hinder such action. Why?

First, in a general sense, states in which revenue generation is not dependent on widespread production in the population are much more susceptible to dysfunction than ones in which the welfare of political elites is closely tied to that of their citizens. Elites are unlikely to promote policies that have an immediate negative effect on their own welfare and survival. Thus, where their welfare is bound up with that of the general population, political and economic elites are more likely to promote policies that advance generalized welfare. Equally true is that widespread production means that the unintended negative effects of policies will be more quickly communicated and matter more to elites. On both of these points, enclave economies hide or displace the costs of destructive economic policies: widespread welfare is not essential to "rent" production, nor does bad policy have an immediately negative effect on that production.

Second, enclave economies do not need functioning states or infrastructure to generate revenues for elites. Here again, enclaves mask, delay, or abrogate the costs of policies that are state-destructive. Take the example, again, of the Democratic Republic of Congo (Zaire) under Mobutu. In this case, "rent" generation was localized to several key mines. To translate mines into revenue, precious little needed to be functioning in the rest of the country. All that was required was mineral extraction and transportation to international markets. Mobutu in reality had few economic incentives to make long-term investments in countrywide infrastructure or in the maintenance of that infrastructure. Nor did Mobutu need a functioning bureaucracy to support the Democratic Republic of Congo's enclave economy. The state as such was quite peripheral to the generation of wealth and revenue. Over time, the country's bureaucracy withered away or served patronage purposes, but it was effectively immaterial to revenue generation. Mobutu's policies were state-destructive, they were unpredictable, and his rule was personal. But these features of personal rule had a structural basis in enclave economies. Neither the state, nor predictability, nor impersonal treatment was crucial to the generation of large amounts of revenue. In a similar fashion, Nigeria's increasing reliance on oil weakened it as a state.[50]

Third, following from the point just made, the form of wealth that enclaves produce supports personal rule. Enclave economies generate a steady stream of lucrative, easily cashed "rents" (taxes and bribes) that can be quickly dispersed to clients and personal networks. Enclave production thus provides the raw material for patronage while doing nothing to build the institutions or incentives that would discourage its widespread use. Taxes on the general populace are unpopular and thus create a negative incentive to balance the political attractions of any patronage they finance. Rents from enclaves are painless to the average citizen, however, and this source of patronage resources therefore bestows nothing but political benefits. Within limits, revenue can be redistributed or pocketed with little immediate economic cost or at least with little risk of destroying the source of the revenue.

Fourth, incentives for encouraging national cooperation or seeking legitimacy are absent in enclave economies, thus again providing a basis for the sustenance of a key feature of personal rule.[51] Where elite and state survival depends on easily captured goods found in small regions and transportable by plane (or easily accessible to ports), domestic bases of support are irrelevant. Far more crucial is direct control over the enclaves that produce wealth. Neither is wealth dispersion a priority. In an economy in which production is multivalent rather than concentrated, state revenue is proportionate to the degree of wealth dispersion.[52] Not so where production is confined to enclaves: there wealth concentration is the norm. In short, enclave production discourages widespread institutional development, popular legitimacy, and wealth dispersion—as well as providing an attractive target for rebel groups.

In these ways, enclave economies facilitate personal rule and all its concomitant features—lack of attention to the public good, unpredictable policy, patronage, and so forth. Enclaves are not the sole cause of personal rule, but they are central to why and how it is sustained over the long run. In Chapter 4, we examine enclave economies in Africa in detail and show how the more extreme among them are highly susceptible to civil conflict.

Personal rule in turn can reinforce the dependence on enclaves. Distribution of "prebends" (offices that are designed primarily to create income for their occupants) encourages state spending, not investment, and contributes to an economically irrational allocation of resources. Lack of predictability also discourages domestic and foreign private investment. The feasibility of these actions is supported by enclave economies. However, their practice carries independent negative economic consequences, which in turn increase enclave dependency and further sap the strength of Africa's weak states—thus reinforcing the two main factors that sustain personal rule in the first place.

Foreign aid reinforces and sometimes substitutes for the effects of enclave production. As with enclaves, overseas development assistance (ODA) creates a system in which state revenue does not depend on a functioning economy. State survival is again disconnected from the productivity of the general population. Not only do detached sources of income facilitate patronage politics and corruption, but they also hinder the development of capable states. A functioning domestic tax structure is one indicator of capable states. Taxes are the backbone of states that are integrated into societies; taxes serve to channel information and link populations to their administrative structures. Foreign aid and enclaves do the opposite: state revenue is detached from the productivity and usually the needs of domestic populations.

Senegal is a useful positive illustration of these points, since its exports are produced by peasants (not enclaves). The politics of the country are dominated by Muslim brotherhoods, whose income is heavily dependent on the export crop production of their members and much less on state patronage. Thus there is an elite that is directly dependent for its welfare on the productive activities of the broad population more than on the extraction of "rents" from natural resources and enclaves. Senegalese politics therefore are more likely to be and are in fact more collectively oriented than the African norm.

By this statement, we do not mean to suggest that there is no corruption in the Senegalese state, that patronage does not still exist, or that electoral behavior is independent of patron-client ties, for all these things remain true. Instead we are suggesting that, compared to most of West Africa, the state has become less central to the personal advancement strategies of elites and that debates on matters of public policy there are driven less by attempts to create "rent-seeking" opportunities than by concern for public policies that would increase the productivity of the farmers on whom the Muslim brotherhoods depend. As a consequence, Senegal has been much more resistant to civil conflict, more open to democratic challenge, and quicker to adopt economic reforms than most of its neighbors. It was early in adopting World Bank economic reforms, and it has displaced a sitting president in a free election. The major factor inhibiting Senegal's movement away from personal rule is foreign aid, which in 1998 still constituted 10.8 percent of its GNP.[53]

In Chapter 2, we examine the negative effects on the combination in Africa of large external debt and dependence on ODA. The enclave-like character of the latter helps to explain the persistence and strength of personal rule in Africa, even in countries that are not strict enclave economies.

Conclusion

International recognition (the "juridical state") combined with enclave production, rather than legitimacy or development, is thus to varying degrees the key to revenue generation for the continent's governments. This political economy essentially dovetails with the continent's historically weak states to sustain personal rule. Elites gain access to the state through patronage; their material advancement largely comes from using the state to collect unearned income (rents) from their government positions or the market niches created by regulations; in turn, the state's rents are generated through the economic regulation of enclaves and foreign aid. The consequence is that states remain weak and detached from their population's productivity. The state does not need deep institutions, capacity, or legitimacy except in small areas. Politics in turn center on a winner-take-all struggle for control of the state as a type of distributional spigot. These distorted incentives are key to the dysfunctional ways in which African states interact with the international system and are at the root of personal rule.

The analysis developed here lends concrete historical and political economy dimensions to the prevalence of personal rule in Africa. Weak states are rooted in the continent's historic interactions with the industrialized world, in particular colonialism and an international state system that rewards formal recognition and hence juridical, not empirical, statehood. This interaction with the international system runs counter to developing capable administrations or national political communities with which to achieve economic development. Although these features tend to be associated with personal rule, we argue that they should be seen as independent from it and as stemming from historical institutional legacies.

Enclave production and to a lesser extent reliance on foreign aid reinforce weak states and provide incentives for other features of personal rule. Although culture, ethnicity, and weak institutions contribute to patronage politics, where the state is a tool for personal gain, the foundation for this system is often its source of revenue. Because of its extreme concentration of single-use assets (asset specificity), enclave production is vulnerable to state predation. This predation facilitates distributional politics in which few incentives for public investment, institutional development, or predictable economic policy exist. To the contrary, enclave production supports politics that are detached from mass publics and are concentrated on the state center, which is the main "rent-collecting" and "rent-distributing" device. Enclave economies and weak states in turn reinforce each other and sustain what is known as personal rule.

In conclusion, the fundamental facts of sub-Saharan Africa today are that its states are weak and that the nature of their economies and their interactions with the international system provide very little incentive for their political elites to make them stronger. Weak states come from Africa's historical and contemporary relationships with the international system. We are not suggesting that the present-day industrial nations that dominate the international system necessarily wish for or even benefit from these dysfunctional relationships. But they are a part of an international system that has these structural effects and therefore must be a part of the solution to Africa's malaise. These premises lead us to a fundamental reappraisal of the efforts of the international system on the continent.

2

Debt and Aid:
Righting the Incentives

M OST SUB-SAHARAN AFRICAN COUNTRIES ARE SADDLED TODAY WITH massive public debts to foreign countries and multinational organizations that they have no prospect of repaying. They are kept from international bankruptcy only by the inflows of aid provided to the continent. The consequences are deeply negative for African development. Much has been made of the ways in which debt may be limiting social expenditures on the continent. Even more important, however, is the fact that the combination of debt and overseas development assistance provides no incentive to African leaders to avoid irresponsible policies and causes them to orient their attentions externally to the international system rather than internally to the productivity and welfare of their own populations. In fact, the current extreme dependence on foreign aid is quite dysfunctional to governance in Africa. The thrust of reform should be to restructure the conditions under which African leaders work, so that there are incentives for better outcomes. It therefore is a high developmental priority for Africa that most of its international debts be written off. It is acceptable and even desirable that this debt cancellation be accompanied by a reduction (but not elimination) of total levels of ODA.

The Magnitude of the Current Debt Crisis in Africa

The World Bank considers that 80 percent of the heavily indebted poor countries (HIPCs) in the world are in sub-Saharan Africa and that 94

21

percent of those African countries have unsustainable levels of debt.[1] The typical HIPC owes international debts that are 126 percent of its GNP and 349 percent of its export earnings.[2] The latter figure is particularly important because these debts are payable in international currencies that can be earned only through exports. Thus to immediately retire its debts, the typical HIPC would have to devote *all* its export revenues to debt repayments for three to four years without receiving *any* imports in return. Not only would the welfare consequences of such a trade be disastrous, but also it would be impossible to accomplish—for it takes imported inputs to produce the exports that these countries sell. For the typical country, it is difficult to see how it could meet even its debt service payments out of its own resources, for they represent 15 percent per annum of its export earnings.[3]

Keeping these debts on the books is deceptive, and no U.S. private bank would be permitted to do so. The debt payments can be met only by providing extremely high levels of aid (ODA) to these countries, which are then recycled abroad again.[4] When the big international private banks faced a similar circumstance in Latin America in the 1980s, they quickly began to sell the debts at deeply discounted prices and by 1990 had written them down by 35 percent.[5] But the multilateral organizations (such as the World Bank) and national governments (such as the United States) that own the publicly guaranteed debts in Africa were much slower to begin forgiving them, despite far less repayment capacity.

Partly this reluctance is due to legal restrictions developed countries have placed on the forgiveness of debts owed to them and the international financial institutions they control. But that begs the question of why these legal restrictions have been maintained in the face of the evident facts that the debts will never be repaid, especially when the international system tacitly accepted widespread default in the similar economic conditions of the 1930s.[6]

There are three parts to the answer. First, many perceive African countries as responsible for their indebtedness and fear that forgiveness of the debt would encourage improvident behavior (i.e., it would create a "moral hazard"). As we will show shortly, this perception is largely false and the fear therefore is exaggerated. Second, the debt crisis of the 1980s threatened the integrity of the banking system of the developed world. Widespread declarations of bankruptcy by developing countries could have brought an economic crisis in industrialized countries. Therefore, the developed north went to great lengths in the 1980s to prevent such declarations.[7] Even if the concern of the industrialized world was selfish, it was valid in the 1980s. But now that the private banks have written down their Latin American debts to manageable levels, the system is no longer threatened, and this concern no longer applies. The debt owed by sub-Saharan Africa is only $230 billion, or 11 percent of the total for low- and middle-income countries.[8] Third, it is thought that debt gives the international financial institutions leverage with which to force African countries to adopt economic policies that are in the best interests of their economies. We will show that although there was much truth in this assumption in the 1980s, it is not valid for the current stage of economic reforms; the disincentives created by debt dependence today far outweigh any positives from the leverage it gives.

The Causes of the Debt Crisis in Africa

The African debt crisis was not due to unusually improvident behavior on the continent. When the Organization of Petroleum Exporting Countries (OPEC) first undertook a significant increase in producer prices in the early 1970s, most analysts and policymakers expected that a global recession would ensue. Instead, the prices of most African commodities boomed, and African governments were able to increase their public expenditures from the dramatic revenue increases. Countries that had borrowed to cope with the oil price shock did well. At the same time, changes in the international banking system made Europe a new source of financing for African countries. Officials, bankers, and especially export credit agencies put together packages for major public investment projects. According to one World Bank study, these projects often were "unproductive, ill-conceived or mismatched with the financing maturity structure. When the second oil price shock hit in the late 1970s, most countries were poorly positioned to absorb it, given their higher level of debt, its less concessional structure, and the inflexibility of public expenditures."[9] The same study showed that the 1980–1983 period aggravated the situation: (1) the second oil shock hurt oil importers; (2) world recession contributed to a decline in export earnings; (3) international real interest rates rose; (4) responses to these negative developments were financed with nonconcessional (i.e., higher-interest) external debt; and (5) drought afflicted many regions.[10] Thus the world slid into the supposedly impossible stagflation combination of no growth, inflation, and high interest rates.[11] Many smart and well-trained economic policymakers were caught out by this turn of events.

The second unexpected development was that the global terms of trade suddenly turned against primary commodities in the 1980s, which also had not been predicted. The prices for the agricultural and mineral products poor countries produced fell 40 percent relative to those for the manufactured goods produced by the industrial economies, which meant that poor countries had to produce more exports for the imported goods they needed to keep their economies functioning. The depressed terms of trade for primary products have continued now for twenty years, creating what we call the "Great African Depression"—one deeper and much longer than the Great Depression of the 1930s in Europe and the United States. For African countries that do not export petroleum, the lower prices for primary exports represented a cumulative loss between 1970 and 1997 of 120 percent of their GDP.[12] Had the relative value of Africa's exports and imports remained at the previous level, the present debts would have been paid off some time ago.

The point, then, is that even well-managed, highly productive developing economies were put under impossible strain in the early 1980s and found themselves facing debts of crisis proportions. This problem was not one of sloth or stupidity. It is true that a number of African countries (such as the Democratic Republic of Congo/Zaire and Nigeria) were irresponsible and corrupt in the debts they assumed. It is also true that most African states, in common with most of the developing world, had adopted import-substituting industrialization (ISI) policies that proved to inhibit economic competitiveness and growth. ISI policies erect a high tariff or quota barrier against imports and thereby create a wall behind which domestic industries can begin to manufacture substitute commodities. Such a policy was used to stimulate "infant industries" in the nineteenth-century United States. In Africa, however, the protections were too extreme and fostered inefficient manufacturing, which was unable to compete internationally and badly distorted local economies. But neither corruption nor ISI were the major source of the African debt crisis, nor do they particularly distinguish Africa from the rest of the developing world.

The debt crisis affected both Latin America and Africa because the international economic system behaved differently than it had before. But Africa almost alone has been left with the consequences because its economies are more dependent on primary product production and its debt was to governmental rather than private bodies. The contrast between Côte d'Ivoire and Mexico is instructive in this regard. Both were similar in their commitment to ISI, and the Mexican government may well have been the more corrupt. Mexico's debt was primarily commercial; Côte d'Ivoire's was public. Most of Mexico's exports are now manufactured goods; Côte d'Ivoire exports primary products, with the consequent vulnerabilities that Paul Collier's research identifies and that were discussed in Chapter 1. Mexico featured prominently in the debt crisis in the 1980s but today is considered secure. The present value of Mexico's debt in 1998 was 39 percent of its GNP, whereas the Côte d'Ivoire was drowning at 120 percent.[13] The difference in the outcomes does not derive from responsibility. In discussing debt relief for Africa, we therefore are not seeking to forgive its leaders for their past sins but to relieve their populations of misfortunes they could not have avoided.

International Leverage

In the 1980s, the World Bank and the International Monetary Fund (IMF) were able to use the debt crisis to gain substantial leverage over economic policy in Africa. Prior to that time, Africa had had less occasion to use the IMF, and World Bank assistance had been strictly limited to project lending. However, the World Bank's 1981 Berg Report created the case for "policy lending," whereby general budget support was given in return for policy reforms.[14] The debt crisis suddenly made this form of assistance very important to African countries. ODA in Africa became equivalent to nearly half of all public spending.[15] (See Table 2.1.) Thus by the end of the 1980s, most African countries had acceded to substantial influence over their economic policies by the Bank and IMF. The net effects of this leverage almost certainly were positive in the 1980s.[16] Although the Bank has been strongly criticized for its neoliberal (free trade, private sector) agenda and the IMF for the negative effects of its deflationary policies on development, the benefits of the devaluation of inflated currencies and the demise of the ISI paradigm are widely accepted.[17]

    The wide acceptance of the less controversial aspects of the IMF and Bank reform agendas in the 1980s and the fact that African growth has *not* recovered has made the wisdom of the international financial institutions' policies for Africa less obvious over the last decade. The

Table 2.1   Aid Intensity in Africa (regional medians of country averages, 1990–1998)

Region/ Country	Real ODA per Capita (1997 $)	Net ODA as Percent of GNP	Net ODA as Percent of Imports[a]	Net ODA as Percent of Investments[a]	Net ODA as Percent of Government Expenditures[a]	Technical Cooperation as Percent of Government Wages
Latin America	20.3	0.4	0.9	3.1	4.5	5.3
South Asia	12.3	4.7	10.5	19.0	46.5	13.2
High-performing Asian countries	3.5	0.1	0.1	0.2	0.2	2.6
Middle East and North Africa	23.1	1.6	2.2	5.2	5.6	3.4
Sub-Saharan Africa	46.1	13.4	25.0	63.5	78.5	17.9
Botswana	85.7	2.9	2.5	5.4	5.6	13.1
Burkina Faso	46.0	17.0	43.5	61.1	78.6	
Cameroon	44.6	5.9	16.6	26.7	44.0	17.9
Mali	50.7	18.3	34.5	58.2	105.8	
Mozambique	76.9	74.3	72.9	218.3	365.0	
Uganda	40.2	16.6	57.1	87.3	157.7	
Zambia	104.5	26.5	37.5	154.6	135.2	

Sources: Stephen O'Connell and Charles Soludo, "Aid Intensity in Africa," *World Development* 29, no. 9 (2001): 1527–1552, tables 5 and 11. See also Carol Lancaster and Samuel Wangwe, *Managing a Smooth Transition from Aid Dependence in Africa* (Washington, D.C.: Overseas Development Council, 2000), p. 13.

Notes: All official development figures (ODA) are net of interest payments. These data do not include private giving by nongovernmental organizations (NGOs) or corporations, which, though still quite small relative to ODA, appears to be increasing in Africa and worldwide. Reliable data on this type of aid are not available. Aid from governments through NGOs is, however, captured in these statistics.

a. Excluding technical assistance.

World Bank has become increasingly critical of the IMF for favoring stabilization at the expense of development, and the Bank has had to make many concessions to the critics of neoliberalism.[18] A good case can be made for neoliberalism. But the same can be said about some of the counterarguments, such as the need for investments in human capital and the dangers of oversupply and falling prices if too many countries pursue an export-led growth strategy with the same primary products. In the context of the predation discussed in Chapter 1, the New Institutional Economics also alerts us to the difficulty of attracting investments in relatively permanent facilities that cannot easily be moved or shifted to other productive purposes (the asset specificity problem). Investors will assume that predation will occur again and factor that calculation into decisions about any capital put into dedicated assets. This problem helps explain the resistance of foreign investors to African markets that appear quite profitable.[19] In this context, simple privatization strategies will not work. Finally, there is substantial evidence that institutional context is much more important to development than neoliberals (free marketers) assumed in the 1980s. Since the institutions that are feasible will be shaped by a country's history, there is no "one best way" to shape market-friendly institutions. The Bank has not necessarily been proven wrong in its policy prescriptions, but there is room for legitimate disagreement and therefore for policy flexibility and experimentation.[20]

Just as important, as the focus of economic reform for Africa has shifted from the easily enforced aspects of macroeconomic policy (such as currency exchange rates) to microeconomic matters of sectoral policy, the ability of the Bank to enforce the conditions on its loans has declined dramatically.[21] For example, the Bank has been striving to get Kenya to liberalize its domestic grain trade without success for twenty years! Any change in the institutional structure of a market is complicated and cannot be delivered overnight. The president of Kenya keeps finding problems with the Bank's prescriptions, promises to study the matter, and never implements a policy product. Independent of the wisdom of the international financial institutions' policies for Africa, their ability to bring them into existence is much more problematic than it was in the 1980s. The leverage granted by the debt crisis has become less valuable. David Dollar and Jakob Svensson and Collier and Gunning both hold that aid volume provides no influence on economic policy today, and the World Bank has publicly accepted their conclusions.[22]

The Domestic Incentives of Debt

Within African countries, the continuation of the debt crisis has created negative incentives for development and the local policymakers who influence it. First, a country with a severe debt burden is a poor risk for direct foreign investment. The investor has to worry if its assets would be depreciated if deflationary debt repayment policies were adopted or if it were otherwise indirectly taxed.[23] Second, once the magnitude of a country's debt rises to a level where it cannot be repaid *no matter what painful changes the country makes,* its policymakers have no incentive to undertake difficult reforms. At the end of the day, the lenders are going to have to pay whatever part of the bill is left; why should the debtors ease them of their burden? From the perspective of the local official, the Bank and the IMF might as well be made to take full political blame for any economic reforms. Furthermore, the implementation of those reforms will be undermined with impunity if there is any short-term gain to doing so. In most African countries, the public blames their current economic difficulties on the World Bank's structural adjustment programs (SAPs) of comprehensive economic reform, not on the various policies of their own governments that helped to produce the economic failures to which SAPs were a response. Their leaders take no responsibility, either for the past or the changes.[24] But many of these same leaders will overspend a budget here or sabotage a reform there if immediate political benefit can be gained by so doing. As bad as this situation is, however, it still is not the entire disincentive created by debt for positive development policy.

Under the current levels of indebtedness, loan payments are possible only through the receipt of very substantial amounts of ODA. The best estimate is that half of all aid to Africa ultimately goes into debt repayments.[25] This aid passes through the hands of local elites in government and nongovernmental organizations (NGOs), where it is easily attached for their benefit, and its amount bears no positive relationship to the country's economic performance. Nicolas van de Walle builds a strong case that African dependence on development assistance has delayed economic reform and reinforced personal rule political systems.[26] Collier and Gunning found a *negative* relationship between economic growth and the amounts of ODA for the great majority of African countries because of their weak policy environments.[27] It is instructive that many African countries receive more in ODA than they collect in tax revenues.[28] Beyond implementing World Bank and IMF economic reforms that are a condition of multilateral aid, local elites have nothing to gain from successfully implementing policies that add to the productive capacity of their economies. By contrast, they have a great deal to gain from continuing aid flows— whether they be from governments or nongovernmental organizations. Thus the debt crisis exacerbates one of the serious structural deficiencies in the political economy of most African states—the fact that local elites have no stake in the productive capacity of most of their brethren.

The Distorted Incentives of Aid

In recent years, the administration and effect of overseas development assistance have received increased international and scholarly attention. In addition to the criticisms found in the works cited above, concern has centered on the negative impact of foreign aid in complex emergencies or humanitarian disasters. The topics of study range from the market effects of food aid during famines to refugee policy to the problems of accountability during conflict.[29] Humanitarian policies toward Rwandan Hutu refugees in the Democratic Republic of Congo after the 1994 genocide focused attention on some negative consequences of foreign aid in complex emergencies. Those policies, which protected armed *genocidaires* and were the root of the first multinational war in the Democratic Republic of Congo, catalyzed calls for a new approach to aid.

The impacts and overall utility of long-term development aid have also received recent attention. Development aid has been the subject of a pair of in-depth studies by the Bank, as well as the subject of several influential scholarly articles.[30] The chief concerns in these studies are whether and how levels of development assistance affect economic policy, whether levels of aid have an appreciable impact on economic growth, and whether levels of aid increase the likelihood of economic reforms being enacted. Subthemes relate to the right composition (technical assistance versus conditional loans, for example, or bilateral versus multilateral), timing of aid (which should come first), and levels of aid (both in terms of how much aid is best relative to policy performance criteria and the levels that distort an economy). In most instances, these studies read as "how to" policy manuals: they seek to improve the overall administration of aid. However, there seems to be a growing recognition that the billions of dollars of aid spent over the last few decades have not translated into concrete improvement in Africa's development prospects and sometimes have had a negative impact.

This increasing attention to and criticism of overseas development assistance is welcome. However, we also would point to a theoretical and practical concern that is independent of the themes identified above and that applies to both emergency and development aid. Aid tends to contribute to and exacerbate the problems associated with enclave production. As with "rentier production," financial flows from aid occur irrespective of widespread economic productivity. In some cases, the relationship is reversed: that is, large problems caused by poverty or a dysfunctional economy lead to calls for higher levels of aid. But even where economies are stable, external financing fuels state budgets and elite salaries. State revenue generation thus does not depend on wealth generation among the population.

In failing to wed domestic productivity to state revenue, the long-term effect of foreign aid is to *decrease* the overall incentives for economic growth. Even if aid is matched to good economic policy, what might be mutually reinforcing links between state and economic development are severed. Indeed, revenue is detached from the population's economic activity, thus increasing the likelihood that distribution will travel through networks of patronage, not productivity, and be subject to predation.

Over time, foreign aid also contributes to weak states. Rather than developing domestically oriented institutions, Africa's state officials orient their actions externally. Indeed, aid can encourage the formulation of plans but not investment in infrastructure. Revenue is tied to state officials' developing statements of intent, which in turn receive funding from external donors. This process also enhances the "quasi-ness" of African states: leaders declare what states will do in order to secure financing but do not necessarily follow through on those plans. Detached from electorates, foreign aid builds in few costs to using aid flows for patronage or corruption. Moreover, aid is vulnerable to donor domestic politics, adding a level of instability and unpredictability that detracts from long-term planning and strategy.[31]

Western aid is sometimes thought of as a restorative response to colonialism and the slave trade. However, Africa's high levels of ODA have effectively extended colonial patterns of governance.[32] Then as now, state survival depends less on socially embedded institutions and more on external funding; policies are oriented toward external, not internal, sources of power; and states operate on "shoestring" budgets, subject to all the misunderstandings and fickleness of the West's relationship to sub-Saharan Africa.

In short, heavy reliance on foreign aid exacerbates Africa's social contract problem. The continent's structure of incentives tends toward accountability to the international system, not to domestic populations. The survival of states and their governing elites rests on external relationships. As with Africa's crippling debt burden, foreign aid extends, rather than counters, the development of responsive and capable states.

Debt Cancellation in Place of Aid

Calls for debt relief for poor countries, particularly those in Africa, have gained prominence and momentum recently. The World Bank has adopted the Heavily Indebted Poor Countries Initiative to forgive the debt of the worst off, which has gained grudging financial support from the U.S. Congress. A group of church and voluntary international development organizations have joined together as Jubilee 2000 to press for much more far-reaching relief. Both endeavors deserve support, but our analysis leads us to ask if either goes far enough.

The World Bank HIPC initiative is limited in two respects. First, it seeks to bring debt to the level where payments are judged to be economically sustainable—but sustainability seems to assume the continuation of ODA. This option leaves in place a structure in which local elites remain independent of the productivity of the local economy and therefore have weak incentives to improve it. Second, by providing for only partial relief and extending it over a number of years, the HIPC initiative is designed to strengthen and continue Bank leverage over African economic policies. Relief is explicitly tied to compliance with the Bank's views of "good" policy over a sustained period.[33] Thus in this respect as well, the initiative neither encourages African elites to be accountable for the performance of their own economies nor permits them to experiment with paths of development outside the neoliberal paradigm.

The program of Jubilee 2000 is more generous and would curtail the leverage of the Bank and IMF. It argues that present levels of ODA provide no net benefit to Africa, once debt payments and expenditures tied to the donor countries are discounted.[34] Although the data on which this calculation was made are not available to us, the conclusion may be correct. And if it is not, the trade-off is certainly close.[35] Nonetheless, Jubilee 2000 still seeks to continue present levels of ODA and therefore would effectively perpetuate the negative incentives of aid dependence.

We would like to argue that not only *could* Africa finance more of its bills for government, welfare, and development if it had complete debt relief but that it *should*. Carol Lancaster and S. M. Wangwe show multiple ways in which the extremely high aid levels in many African countries (Table 2.1) can distort their economies.[36] In the 1970s Africa asked for "trade, not aid." It now might well ask for "autonomous development, not aid." The cancellation of Africa's debts by itself would make it a much better investment risk and would create the incentives for local elites to adopt the policies that would make it more so.[37]

We said Africa "might well ask," not "does ask," however. Africa's elites would dearly love to have autonomy once again from the international system, but most would not be happy to surrender their dependence on ODA to achieve it. The risks and challenges that go with being responsible for and dependent on the performance of a national economy are not trivial, and not all elites are equally prepared to take advantage of the new incentives the change would create. Indeed, significantly reducing levels of foreign aid and writing off debt would require a fundamental restructuring of relations between governments and societies in Africa. The current levels of ODA actually create a major source of patronage to sustain Africa's personal rule systems.[38] A reduction in ODA would upset existing governance practices and, we believe, lead governing elites to orient policies toward developing more productive economies and states embedded in domestic sources of legitimacy. Such a reorientation would create new winners and losers and thus would not be easy. But these are precisely the reasons why the trade-off between debt and aid is necessary.

That said, however, we are *not* arguing for a cessation of ODA for Africa. We do think it would be valuable to reduce it in return for cancellation of all (or at least most) debt. We also think it would be well to end "policy lending" and general budgetary support for African countries. But continuation of some forms of assistance is needed to cope with the magnitude of the refugee and the health crises in Africa, the latter particularly but not exclusively from AIDS. To keep incentives properly aligned, however, the assistance that addresses these problems needs to be carefully targeted in ways that keep elites dependent on their own economies. The challenge is to redirect the remaining forms of ODA toward welfare and to return to Africans themselves the responsibility for making decisions about their own development.[39]

Nor would a dramatic reduction in ODA necessarily harm Africa's poor. Since at least half of current ODA flows back out of Africa in debt payments, halving ODA in conjunction with debt cancellation would have no effect on *net* transfers to most countries—but it would reduce the points at which money can be siphoned off by African administrators. From the point of view of welfare, the important challenge is to be sure that the ODA that does remain is channeled toward the sick and the poor.

It might be objected that as long as there is *any* significant ODA, the marginal benefits to receiving it will exceed the marginal effort needed to obtain it and therefore will continue to shape the advancement strategies of local elites. We disagree and think the size of the aid pie matters. At the moment, ODA in most of sub-Saharan Africa is so pervasive that it dominates the thinking of the whole *class* of local elites. As the amount of aid diminishes, some elites will continue to focus on ODA, but a larger and larger percentage of the class will turn its attention to other paths for achievement.

Feasibility

Canceling debt and significantly reducing aid require major changes in the way the international system approaches Africa. If some African leaders will balk at ending aid dependence, Western governments too are likely to hesitate at restructuring their relationships to African states. How feasible, then, are the proposals advanced here?[40]

The strongest opposition to debt forgiveness for Africa seems to be motivated by fears that anything resembling national bankruptcy proceedings would weaken the international financial system. This concern appears to be especially strong in Japan. We note that once again, the interests of the developed world are driving policies toward Africa. And different standards have been applied to the "moral hazards" created by helping the big banks out of their improvident behavior. Instead, we would suggest that writing off most or even all of these loans after they have created twenty years of severe economic hardship does not create much incentive to embrace such moral hazards in the future. The punishment already meted out has been sufficiently harsh to warn later leaders from going down the same path. Renewed stability and growth in Africa also will reduce strains on the international system and create enhanced economic benefits for the industrial world.

Despite the strength of the arguments for full debt relief, however, the international financial community is likely to insist on some fig leaf of repayment. The most substantial officially sanctioned debt relief in modern times occurred in 1942, when Mexico was permitted to write off all but 10 percent of its obligations.[41] Even this is more than what is being made generally available through the HIPC initiative. The crucial point is that debt needs to be written down to levels at which further payments are easily feasible without *any* ODA—even if aid for poverty and crisis alleviation continues. Thus feasibility needs to be assessed on the assumptions that there is no aid bolstering the "exports" side of the national accounts and that any *new* loans will be at market rates. Autonomy will then be regained, and future ODA will be genuine welfare, not pass-through payments to creditors.

Some have advocated that instead of cancellation, ownership of the debts should be transferred from foreign organizations to local NGOs, as a way of giving the latter more leverage over local political systems. We think this solution could be dysfunctional, for it would transfer dependency to a new site. Who would choose the beneficiaries among the self-appointed NGOs, and who would protect their new economic power from the local states? A new form of externally oriented conditionality would be introduced, and these countries already are suffering from too much dysfunctional conditionality.

Thus the other major issue concerning debt relief is the amount of conditionality that accompanies it. The incentives governing national elites will be distorted as long as opportunities for official and nongovernmental aid dominate their horizons. If the alternative for a member of the local economic or social elite is to devote attention to obtaining government patronage rather than ODA, then it is plausible (although not necessarily true) that donor conditions and incentives would do more to foster economic development. But if the alternative is direct economic activity, it is very unlikely that the average donor provides incentives that are more appropriately aligned to the economy than the market does. For this reason, some risk in the exchange of aid reduction for debt relief is acceptable. It is true that governing elites who have deeply ingrained commitments to the worst forms of personal rule and its attendant economic policies will not respond quickly to the new incentives, and their countries therefore are poor targets for the exchange we advocate. Where there has been a transition from a deeply patronage-ridden and corrupt regime to new modes of governing, however, it is important to move quickly from the old relationships of conditionality and dependence to the new patterns of autonomous responsibility.

Some will argue that the patronage patterns of Africa's personal rule systems are deeply ingrained and thus that assuming leaders will respond appropriately to the new incentives is risky. It *is* a risk. But the present system of debts, conditionality, and aid dependence is a demonstrated failure. A risky positive is preferable to a proven negative. We do hope that questionable loans become more difficult to obtain and those that are made are more closely tied to development. Massive new indebtedness would be disastrous. The power to determine new levels of indebtedness lies with international actors; one can only hope that the lessons of the 1970s to the 1990s have been learned and that pressure will come to bear on obviously harmful loans—including, for example, those for large weapons procurements.

Ending crushing debt and sharply curtailing aid represent the best way forward for the international system for several reasons. First, stability and economic development in Africa are in the security and material interests of the West. Instability and poverty in Africa over time will have a negative impact on the rest of the world. Second, to the extent that the international system's current engagement stems from a normative commitment to development, searching for solutions that would reverse current trends on the continent remains an imperative. Third, African development is a beneficial outcome in itself—one that electorates, even if vocal minorities, in comparatively wealthier countries will support. Canceling most of the debt and reducing aid are crucial steps that will restructure incentives, leading to the development of more capable states, improvements in African governments' social contracts with their citizens, and over time stability and economic growth.

Conclusion

We find that both international debt and dependence on unusually large levels of foreign aid have severely hampered African development. Together they have grossly distorted the incentives driving African political and economic elites and have created a dynamic inimical to development. The foreign debt of all but the seriously corrupt African states should be promptly cancelled. In return, ODA for Africa probably would be halved—with *positive* development effects. The result would be an Africa that once again has gained sovereign control over and responsibility for its economic development.

3

Technical Assistance:
The Corrosion of Unwitting
Institutional Racism

THE AFRICAN CAPACITY FOR DEVELOPMENT MANAGEMENT IS SERIOUSLY deficient. About this point, there is little controversy.[1] The problem is how to remedy the shortcomings. Despite the substantial resources devoted to it since 1960, development management in Africa has not improved. It is safe to say that any strategy for building African development management capacity that relies exclusively or even primarily on formal training will fail. Moses Kiggundu speaks for many when he says that training institutions "have not had a significant impact on management development in Africa."[2] It is time to rethink the development management problem from first principles and to see if there may not be additional tools for addressing it that together with training offer a better prospect for making substantial progress. In this chapter, we argue that tacit (or informal) learning now must assume priority over formal training and, even more fundamentally, that rather than focus exclusively on the supply of managerial talent, serious distortions in the demand for effective African development managers and the incentives under which they operate must be corrected. The problem is *not* the capacity of Africans for development management but a set of structures and incentives that inhibit its expression.

This chapter was researched and written by David K. Leonard.

The Requisites to Effective Development
Management in Africa

"Effective development management" is the complex of behaviors by the leaders of an organization that enable it to make a significant contribution to economic development. There are multiple ways in which development can be defined and pursued, and our discussion here is neutral between them. But development management serves a public good and does *not* include effectiveness in the pursuit of purely private goals, or even of political objectives, that detract from economic development.

In reality, public management is not one thing but many. So it would be well if we began by acknowledging the plurality of the phenomena and the tensions that sometimes exist between them. David Leonard's research over the years on effective development management in Africa suggests that four different types of management behavior are involved—public policy making, organizational leadership, internal administration, and what we will call "bureaucratic hygiene."[3] These activities are not at all the same; what is more, excellence in one of them frequently can be purchased at the expense of one of the others.

1. *Public policies,* of course, are the most important way in which a state affects development. They are important issues of public management because they are among the most critical variables affecting program success and sustainability. For example, agricultural development programs will be for naught if commodity prices are publicly set at an unprofitable level.

2. *Organizational leadership* is the second variety of management. It entails setting goals and the mobilization of the human and material resources necessary to achieve them. The largest part of a leader's efforts is probably directed at factors that are external to his (or her) organization: funds and authorizations are secured; the cooperation of other agencies is negotiated; the support of clients is obtained; and political threats to a program's image and mission are averted. Even many of the internal aspects of a leader's task are political in character—obtaining consensus on goals, inspiring commitment, negotiating interunit conflicts, and so on. This part of management is an art, not a science, and it is second only to public policy in determining whether a project or program will be successful.

3. *Internal administration* is what we usually think of as management. It entails the organization of work and already secured resources

to achieve agreed-upon goals. As important as it is, it is clearly subordinate in importance to a congenial policy framework, an appropriate set of goals, and the acquisition of resources to administer.

4. *Bureaucratic hygiene*. Particularly in the public sector, internal administration also requires the operation of certain control systems that have been designed to assure those outside the organization that its resources are not being misused (e.g., accounts, audits, civil service regulations, contracting mechanisms, and administrative law). These functions, which might be said to maintain "bureaucratic hygiene," are not directly productive themselves. Organizations that are *too* scrupulous about them may fail to meet their objectives because of goal displacement. But it also is true that those that do badly on them often have difficulty securing and managing the resources they need. Donors, for example, are unlikely to entrust them with funds unless they are monitored by their own technical assistance personnel (what John M. Cohen has called "gate-keeper advisers").[4]

When we consider the factors that affect the success of programs and projects, the hierarchy of importance begins with public policy, is followed by leadership and general internal administration, and ends with bureaucratic hygiene. For example, Barbara Grosh found that policy problems account for much of the poor performance of Kenyan public corporations.[5] In a comparative study of public corporations in Botswana and Tanzania, Rwekaza Mukandala concludes that performance is largely determined by the political context and government agenda within which these corporations operate.[6] By extension, the same argument that performance problems are based in the framework of public policy applies to the regular government ministries as well. Are we then to conclude that management accounts for little in the variation in effectiveness of these organizations?

Grosh's and Mukandala's analyses imply that policymaking and management are separable functions. They are not. Philip Selznick's 1957 classic, *Leadership in Administration,* stressed that the most important role of chief executives is not internal administration but setting the objectives for their organizations and mobilizing the resources to achieve them.[7] This view was presaged in the work of Chester Barnard[8] and has been strongly reinforced by organizational studies done since.[9] It is reflected in the way in which we just defined management.

Effective administrators are not the passive recipients of public policies but exhibit leadership and skill at manipulating the environment of their organizations.[10] The best managers actively shape the policy framework within which they operate, even though they operate in constrained environments and do not always win their policy struggles. Successful managers focus on the issues that are central to their organization's performance and assemble the resources necessary to address them. To the extent that those issues are matters of public policy, they seek to find politically viable policy alternatives, to present them cogently to those with the power to influence their acceptance, and to mobilize support for them.

Management does make a difference. It sets direction and secures external resources and policies. It also is needed to focus the organization's internal energies and motivates and empowers the efforts of subordinates. Organizational leadership thus has both external and internal faces.

If management does matter, then what makes a good manager? The following observations are based both on the research of others and on our own interviews with Kenyan civil servants about the attributes they considered to be important in the managerial successes of others in Africa.[11]

1. *Political connections and organizational autonomy.* One of the older pieces of wisdom on government organizations, particularly public corporations, is that their effective management requires political autonomy. The autonomy of an organization from undue politicization is not something that can simply be granted to it even in a constitutional act. It has to be earned and then maintained through political connections. As is illustrated by the work of Mukandala and Grosh, virtually all public organizations need favorable policy decisions and additional resources at critical junctures if they are to prosper.[12] They also need protection from unwise policy initiatives and politicization. All these requisites, even depoliticization, are achieved as a consequence of political action. In most African states, the relevant political intervention comes from the president. Effective public servants are able to mobilize support at critical junctures *not* by building independent political bases of support for themselves or their organizations but from personal access to and the confidence of the president, either directly or through others who are close to him or her.

2. *Professional concern with public policy and organizational mission.* Not everyone who has the confidence of a president is going to use it to advance the performance of the organization that he or she

leads. This is particularly true for those who come to positions of leadership in Africa through a political career or because of their ability to mobilize support in the larger political community. They are apt to see their positions and the powers that they convey as a reward for the delivery of their support to the president, not as a resource to be used to advance the effectiveness of the organization. Managers with this type of political support tend to sap, not strengthen, their units.

However, the problem goes well beyond politicians. John D. Montgomery's study of southern African managers left him troubled about the ends toward which they were administering their organizations. Development goals did not play a prominent role in their decisions and activities. Money and turf were the most frequent causes of bureaucratic conflict; policy matters came a distinct fifth. When resources were at stake, "there is not much concern over their relation to their public origin or to the public interest. . . . Arguments . . . center about the convenience of the individual users more than about the mission of the organization to which they are assigned."[13]

Effective development managers differ quite dramatically from this characterization. They have very well defined organizational missions that they want to accomplish, are activist and entrepreneurial in their pursuit, devote considerable attention to the public policies affecting them, and attempt to serve the public interest. They see internal administration as grounded in a larger set of purposes and feel some responsibility as well for the factors outside their organization that affect them. Leonard's research suggests that these attributes come from committed professionalism.

3. *Professional integrity.* Effective development managers place the interests of the organizations they serve above their own pursuit of personal gain. The general political and social environment of which managers are a part in Africa often is quite unconcerned about corruption and effectively encourages it. In much the same way as Robert Price demonstrated for Ghana, the question in the popular mind usually is not how prominent officials get their wealth but whether they are personally transferring resources to their relatives and home areas.[14] A different set of values usually prevails *inside* public agencies in Africa, among the professional subordinates and peers of development managers. The respect and support that a manager of a professional organization receives from his or her subordinates and peers in related organizations appears to be heavily contingent on his or her perceived personal integrity. This does not mean that these subordinates and peers

are always behaving with integrity themselves. Unlike members of the general public, however, they understand the concept of conflict of interest and feel that they owe effort and support to those who are faithful to it, even if they are not. Conversely, they feel free to be slack in their duties if they are asked to do something by someone whose integrity they doubt.

Note, then, that "effective management" is not a foreign concept in Africa. It is already present inside bureaucracies, at least in a nascent form. The challenge is to restructure the incentives under which managers work so that this concept of professionalism takes priority over the dysfunctional concepts of personal rule that prevail politically and among the general public.

4. *Access to donor resources.* Another attribute that proves critical to managerial effectiveness is the ability to inspire the confidence of international actors. African economies are relatively small and weak, and international markets, together with gifts and loans from international donors, are unusually important to them. Those managers who are skilled at acquiring these resources are able to use them to gain flexibility in an environment that is usually severely constrained. They also perform a function for the economy that gives them support from other powerful domestic politicians and public servants.

5. *Africanization.* Frequently there is a down side to donor confidence, one that reduces the loyalty that managers inspire in their own staff. Effective development managers sometimes feel that they have to use some nonlocal staff to maintain high professional standards in their organizations, standards that give them a strong international reputation. The morale and allegiance of their local staff depend, however, on a vigorous Africanization program that replaces foreign with local staff. Those who handle this dilemma best tend to concentrate expatriate staff in training positions and in those parts of the organization where new functions are being added. They also try to externalize the conflict, suggesting that the expatriate presence will enable the organization to impose a local agenda in the face of international pressure. They are then able to rally nationalist sentiment for their personnel policies despite the continued use of foreigners.

6. *Being a "nationalist."* Not only is the nationalism inherent in the pressures to Africanize directed against foreigners; it also is a force against undue parochialism in the allocation of resources, particularly those related to employment. All public institutions in Africa employ a mixture of ethnic groups throughout their hierarchy. If the organization

is to perform effectively, these ethnically diverse staff must be able to work well together. Not only will a manager typically have to rely on the efforts of crucial subordinates who do not belong to his group, but a staff member also usually finds that the hierarchy that controls his or her promotion has someone from another group in it somewhere.

The pattern of values with regard to ethnic favoritism is similar to the one for corruption. Society expects that senior administrators will provide assistance to those from their home areas and applies a good deal of pressure toward that end. Civil servants also expect such behavior from their colleagues, but unlike the general society, they are ambivalent about it. Many use junior staff appointments they control to satisfy the pressures of petitioners from their villages, and some try to find ethnic allies to help them promote their own careers, although usually without too much success. But these same civil servants do not want to see signs of parochialism among their own superiors. They expect it but admire its absence. A superior who is a "nationalist" commands their respect and commitment. The organization then performs well. Superiors who are parochial are given only the cooperation that they can coerce and are often undermined by those outside their group.

7. *Staff management.* Africanization and nationalism are really Africa-specific attributes of the more universal issue of staff management. Effective development managers set high standards for their staff, which involves having clear expectations for work to be done and holding staff responsible for results. But staff management is also staff development.[15] The kinds of personal rewards provided and loyalties developed through close attention to this function are important to organizations everywhere. But they may be especially important in Africa, where the *institutional* standards and incentives are often weak.

8. *Risk taking.* A further attribute that emerges from case studies of effective development managers is the willingness to take risks, an attribute that seems to be rare among African managers.[16] Only the risk takers will assume challenging tasks, push the agendas of their superiors, be unorthodox in solving problems, and protect their talented subordinates when they are unfairly criticized. It appears that the existence of career alternatives outside the local civil service gives managers the confidence necessary to take risks.

Now that we have sketched some of the conclusions of the empirical literature on the determinants of effective African development management, the question becomes, "How can this capacity be created—or at least stimulated and supported?"

The Multiple Factors Involved in the Creation of Effective African Management

From the point of view of those wishing to enhance African managerial performance, the ability of a manager to inspire presidential confidence is an exogenous variable over which they can have little influence. All outsiders can do is ensure that the other attributes of managerial effectiveness are widely distributed, increasing the probability that someone who has them will also be close to the president. Of these other attributes, three are of greatest importance and are in fact related to one another. Concern with organizational mission, professional integrity, and risk taking are all influenced by professionalization. A manager who is deeply imbued with the values of his or her profession is focused on organizational goals and keeps his or her own interests from interfering with their pursuit. Furthermore, someone with internationally recognized professional qualifications, standing, and reputation has a wide range of options as to how and where he or she can earn a living and therefore is in a good position to take risks.

The value socialization imparted in the process of professional education must be reinforced if it is to be sustained over time. The individuals who enter these professions must identify with these values and look to their fellow professionals for reward. Thus we must look at the informal processes surrounding work and the larger set of incentives shaping the ways people perform on the job.

Supply Factors

Strong professional training is desirable, then, not just because it teaches skills but also because it socializes. The techniques and methods of analysis that are learned have public-regarding values embedded within them. In addition, a network of professional connections fosters autonomy, and the possession of a recognized credential permits risk taking. Best at this socialization are the traditional professions, such as medicine, engineering, accounting, and law, all of which have clear minimum training requirements for membership, which often are internationally recognized. Economics also has imbedded public-regarding values, although it lacks recognized entry qualifications.[17]

Cohen dissents from the view that recognized professional credentials are desirable. In his experience in Kenya, once civil servants had been helped to obtain such credentials, they quickly departed the public service for better-paying positions elsewhere. This problem is widespread in contemporary Africa. Cohen's Harvard technical assistance projects in Kenya responded by providing highly focused training programs that did not lead to recognized credentials; staff who had been through such programs had more difficulty using them to stimulate outside offers and therefore were more likely to stay in the civil service and enhance its capacity.[18] This use of formal training to create professional values without facilitating civil service flight is ingenious and may well be necessary in many settings. Nonetheless, it is a decidedly second-best solution. It purchases commitment by reducing outside options and therefore will discourage risk taking. The attractiveness of Cohen's strategy arises only from the serious inadequacy of the incentives being offered to skilled people to continue in civil service careers. Cohen would concur that the preferable solution would be to have adequate salaries for professional staff in government (although he was pessimistic about the likelihood of meaningful change).[19]

Whatever one's position on the desirable types of formal training, the real focus of attention now needs to be on implicit training and tacit learning. There is wide consensus that managers learn most and best on the job. In Peter Blunt and Merrick Jones's investigation of managerial thinking in Malawi, for example, "when asked how they learned their managerial abilities, respondents named 'learning by doing the job' as the most important influence, followed by 'discussing real problems with colleagues,' 'training by boss,' 'observing effective managers,' and 'analyzing my successes and failures.'"[20] The amount of attention that has been given to this aspect of capacity building has been seriously deficient.

Individuals need to have opportunities for extended work experience in organizational settings where work is being done effectively and they are being rewarded for the quality of their own work. Good salaries may purchase good managers, but they will not create them. Only the combination of incentives and strong organizational settings can accomplish this goal.

Prospective managers need tacit learning in functional organizations. It is very hard for them to learn positive lessons in dysfunctional organizations, and those lessons they do learn will not be reinforced. Cohen provides a sad catalogue of the multiple ways in which poor staff management can stifle the environment for tacit learning of managerial skills. It is plausible that an impact on capacity building could be achieved indirectly by holding a series of high-level seminars to train the most senior African officials themselves how to manage their staff so as to build and manage the capacity of their subordinates. Even at this level, however, a background of tacit learning in functional organizations is desirable.[21]

Professionals are not produced and certainly are not sustained simply through the exposure of individuals to professional training. The mastery of technique *and* the socialization in professional norms that are provided through this training are of critical importance. But training and socialization alone will not sustain the candidate professional in the face of strong contrary pressures in the environment.

Only when the candidate professional has other professionals as an important (if not the most important) reference group in his or her work life will he or she be transformed into a true professional. The group of peers provides the social structure that permits the professional to resist the otherwise powerful pressures to fall short of professional norms.

In an ideal situation, the professional association would formally sanction or bar someone who violated professional standards. Even short of formal sanctions, however, the existence of informal criticism from a group of people whom one respects and identifies with is a powerful social sanction.

In most of Africa, however, the indigenous professional community is too small and too weak to fulfill this peer group function effectively alone. In this circumstance, the professional association is likely to be only a self-enhancing status group, if it exists at all. Only those individuals who are strongly oriented toward the *international* profession and see their international peers as a central reference group for their behavior are likely to behave appropriately. Nascent respect for these professional values *is* present already in the professionalized parts of the bureaucracy, but the incentives against their guiding personal behavior are too strong for them to be effective without outside support.

To strengthen African professions, strong links to international professional organizations are needed. To begin with, this requirement implies that a relatively substantial number of African professionals would actively participate in their relevant international professional associations and gatherings—not just the present token numbers.

Also implied is the involvement of the relevant international professional organization in national certification and in-service training functions, until such time as the counterpart national association is able to cross a certain threshold in standards, size, and autonomy. African professionals will be rightly insulted at any implication that they are any less dedicated to standards than their international compatriots. But that is not the issue. The point instead is that Africa's professional associations at the moment are not closely connected to the academic centers that are generating new professional knowledge. In addition, they are too small and fragile to be able to withstand the substantial political and social pressures put on them in their home countries, which threaten their integrity and autonomy. African professionals need connections and support to meet the professional standards *to which they themselves aspire*. International links can help them accomplish this goal.

The Interdependence of Supply and Demand

Capacity building for African development management has been dominated by "supply-side economics." Initially, this course was appropriate. When African states first achieved their independence, they were faced with the task of quickly filling large numbers of public management positions that had formerly been occupied by expatriate officers from the metropoles. Because of colonial discrimination, too few Africans had comparable skills, and the challenge was to provide the training that would build these numbers up. Forty years later, however, it is implausible that the nature of the problem is the same. A full generation of African civil servants has come and gone. If African managers still are not adequate to their tasks, something more than formal training has been missing.

The distorted market for development managers in Africa has dampened the demand for *effective and skilled* Africans to fill these positions. When demand for good managers is strong, it not only generates the prices (salaries) that will draw people to these positions from other posts but also creates the incentives to undertake training and the motivation for learning and internalizing the lessons it offers. Without effective demand for the skills that training is trying to foster, the learning process is leached of its motivating energy. Students may be anxious for the *credentials* training offers if promotions are based on formal qualifications, but they will not be interested in mastering the content of the lessons if the skills that are being imparted are not being rewarded for their own sake. In the present era, a supply-side approach to capacity building is like pushing on a string. Until there is a demand-side pull, nothing will be moved.

Moses Kiggundu makes the same basic point in somewhat different language:

> Focusing on a single human resource activity like training without systematic analysis of its relationships with other internal or external dimensions of the organization can be unproductive or even counterproductive. . . . Most discussions of human resource management in developing countries focus on human resource development but virtually neglect human resource utilization.[22]

The decline in African development management has occurred for two reasons: African civil servants have inadequate incentives to be effective development managers (as the larger development community defines effectiveness), and the informal processes whereby African public officials can engage in the tacit learning of the skills necessary to effective management have been either distorted or destroyed.

Can it be true, when the clamor for African development managers is nearly universal, that the demand for their skills is weak? Yes, because the real demand is distorted in a number of important ways. At present, African managers in most states will not receive sufficient income to reproduce themselves (i.e., to raise their children to be able to occupy positions at a level in society equivalent to their own) if they are honest, effective, and remain in the public sector.

One part of the problem, in some states, is political leaders who are more interested in seeing public offices manipulated to generate patronage benefits for themselves and their clients than they are in seeing effective management in the broader public interest. Even where political leaders are not personally corrupt, however, public sector salaries for managers in Africa are notoriously inadequate at present. The politics of equity and the resulting wage compression prevents these leaders from openly paying their top managers the kinds of incomes they usually could achieve elsewhere. Why, then, do these civil servants remain in the public sector? In the present circumstances of a large number of African countries, senior and talented personnel are encouraged to remain in government through a variety of side payments rather than salaries. Some of the side payments—government housing, chauffeur service, special access for families to places in more attractive schools and medical facilities—cleverly get around the politics of wage equality without having negative effects on the nature of the work done. But others produce quite perverse incentives and have become more important.

When senior jobs produce opportunities to collect bribes, to evade income-inhibiting restrictions on one's private trade, to win government contracts for one's family or associates, or to misappropriate public funds, incentives are created to do one's job in ways that are not consistent with the public interest. These practices represent a return to practices of "tax farming" and "benefices," which used to dominate Western and East Asian administration and were eliminated with great difficulty but substantial benefit over the last two centuries. As long as these methods of attracting skilled personnel remain, the public and donors alike will have good reason to doubt the integrity of the decisions made by African senior civil servants.

Managers must be persuaded (which means it must be true) that they actually will be able to do better for their extended families in the long run if they eschew nepotism and other "benefits" and do their jobs effectively and in the public interest. That is what economists mean by getting incentives "correctly aligned."

Note that the problem is not simply one of getting salaries high enough to attract talented people to the civil service and getting them to stay there. The problem, in addition to attracting the physical presence of the people with the right skills and potential, is to give them the incentives to do their jobs effectively and honestly (and to master the informal skills for them to be able to do so). Without this added feature, development will not be achieved and donors will not be willing to replace expatriate personnel (who *are* subject to such incentives) with African managers.

If the analysis were to stop here, one might conclude that the perverse politics of many contemporary African states makes it impossible to provide adequate incentives to induce public development managers to do an effective job. Within the narrow boundaries of many African political systems, this conclusion may be true. But there are other important resources and actors within these national systems.

Technical Assistance

Through technical assistance, donors spend substantial sums for development managers. However, the way these resources are used inhibits their having the maximum effect possible. Donors deal with the shortage of skilled, local development managers by importing expatriates at salaries prevailing in the industrialized world. But at the time of decolonization, they also established the principle that these high salaries would not be offered to local staff, who preferably were to be employed by their own governments and in any case were to be reimbursed at local wage levels. It was the correct decision at the time. The supply shortages of local managers at that time were severe, indigenous salary scales for managers (although low by international standards) were very attractive, and an increase in demand through higher wages would not have produced more local talent. It was more appropriate to relieve the supply shortage by expanding training opportunities and keeping local managerial salaries at sustainable levels.

The picture is different today. Although the standards of many African institutions of higher education have declined, the numbers graduating both at home and abroad are now large enough to meet the demand at the level of formal qualifications. The problem instead is that those who combine these qualifications with the capability and interest to work effectively no longer see a career devoted to public service as capable of meeting their lifetime income needs. Nor do those who do enter the civil service have much incentive to learn how to be effective in their jobs once they have been hired.

The harsh truth is that the two-track salary system created by international development assistance today is a form of institutional racism. Although there are people of color, including foreign and occasionally local Africans, serving in technical assistance roles, the overall workings of the system sustain higher wages for the (generally white) citizens of industrial countries and privilege their employment over that of well-qualified locals. Given that this system also has distorted the local incentive system, it is imperative that it be fundamentally restructured.

Technical assistance is not about to pass into obsolescence of its own accord. Incredibly enough, the number of technical assistance personnel in Africa today is *higher* than in the years after independence, when the numbers of trained locals were low.[23] Given that these expatriate staff are substantially more expensive than locals, they create not only a problem but also an opportunity. If effective incentive systems for local managers can be created, the programs can be financed from the savings generated by phasing out the foreigners.

Alternatives

In thinking about incentives, it is important to focus on the individual manager's full career. Many developed countries recognize that they cannot provide adequate incentives to keep top people in civil service positions and find ways around this problem. France and Japan reward civil servants for outstanding public service in the first half of their careers by getting them lucrative parastatal and private sector positions afterward. The United States takes people who have already used the private sector to meet their career income ambitions and attracts them back into public service with the promise of prestige, public attention, and a sense of having influence on and serving the public good.

In Africa, it may well be inevitable that eventually almost all talented people will leave the civil service for well-remunerated jobs elsewhere. The critical thing is to make sure that they do good and appropriate work in the civil service in order to qualify for and get those external opportunities. If they get access to external opportunities based on their training, they have no incentive to do a good job. It is important that these external opportunities be recognized for what they are—important incentives—and used accordingly.

Even with a career perspective, however, the salaries of senior civil servants in many African countries are so low that it is hard to keep good managers in their posts for even half their careers. L. S. Wilson has countered that topping up salaries or other inducements for public managers will not do very much to increase the supply of people with the desired formal qualifications (at least in the short and intermediate run). On this point, he is right. He goes on to suggest that such salaries will work primarily to shuffle talent around and out of the private sector. This latter argument misses an important part of the point, however. There are many people in these economies already who have the formal qualifications necessary for effective development management but who are not being effective (because they lack the incentives). A change in incentives could lead to a rapid change in the ways in which formally qualified people *behave*. (This point applies to managers, not policy analysts, for whom skills learned in formal training institutions are much more important. Also, these new people would not necessarily be as good as the best technical assistance personnel, who often are recruited from a very wide base and have received outstanding formal and informal training in some of the best institutions in the world. The suggestion instead is that the right incentives could provide locals, say, three-fourths as good as the modal technical assistance personnel at, say, one-half the price.) In other words, the right combination of incentives would significantly increase the supply of managers with the attributes of professionalism, integrity, "nationalism," and good staff management that we identified above as critical.

The amounts of money going into technical assistance in Africa are large enough to have a significant impact on the incentives under which African senior civil servants work if they are intelligently managed. Countries must use donor resources to top-up the salaries of selected public servants in (1) a potentially sustainable way so as (2) to reward and retain outstanding local managers and (3) to expand the pool of local managerial talent, (4) without simply adding to the pool of resources that are corruptly traded within the system.

Meeting these four objectives simultaneously will be difficult. The second criterion is not hard to meet; many donors have already begun to provide formal and informal incentives to keep critical local personnel at work on their projects.[24] The ad hoc nature of the present donor response, however, frequently has made the other goals more difficult to meet. If donor-provided inducements are not integrated into public sector salary scales, managers only jump from one donor project to another, and no local capacity is ever generated. Such donor behavior implicitly says that the only real priorities for the public sector are donor ones.

Similarly, if the topping-up arrangements offered with donor support provide substantially better wages than those available to effective managers on the (public and private) market, the temptation to trade these positions corruptly is overwhelming. Integrity—one of the crucial attributes of effective development management—is then undermined, and organizational morale and performance still declines.

Donor inducements have to be put into the system in such a way that local civil servants can see a real *career* in learning and practicing professional development management. Donor resources have to be made to reward local managers in a *systematic, reliable, and institutionalized way*. It is safe to say that at present that is being done rarely, if at all.

Two alternative proposals for achieving the four objectives for an incentive system are given in the appendixes. Another set of proposals has been made by Elliot Berg and his colleagues in *Rethinking Technical Cooperation: Reforms for Capacity Building in Africa*. The latter's methods are still too ad hoc to meet the above four objectives and create a systematic, reliable, and institutionalized system. However, any one of these three proposals or a variant on them would be an improvement on the current situation. We need African policymakers and donors themselves to make the choice among them so that they own the results.

Both of the proposals in the appendixes seek to narrow the gap between technical assistance and local salary scales and to raise local performance standards closer to international ones. In the first (as presented in Appendix A), local public service commissions adopt the principle that when individual civil servants receive outside job offers and when their superiors wish to retain their services, their local salaries will be adjusted upward to provide a competitive wage. Similarly, when people are hired into the civil service from the outside, their local pay would be set to have equivalent real value to what they were earning before. When a high percentage of the members of a job group were receiving off-scale salaries, the pay scale for the entire job group would be adjusted upward. Under such a system, the most effective way for local civil servants to increase their salaries would be for them to perform their duties in ways that impressed international employers and led to good job offers. In effect, this practice would import and reinforce international performance standards into the local system and reduce the incentive to use one's job as a "prebend"—an opportunity to collect "bribes" from one's clients rather than to provide service. Because the only civil servants receiving competitive matches to outside offers would be those whom their supervisors wished to retain, those remaining in local employment would be responsive to the policy objectives of national political leaders. A civil service system that operated in this way would have a higher wage bill than the current ones do—but probably not prohibitively so. Only high performers would receive the benefit, and as their numbers grew, so would the effectiveness of the local administrative system. Once a market principle for salary adjustments was accepted, the pressure for across-the-board wage increases would be reduced. To the extent that such a system did cost more, it would be a worthwhile investment for donors to subsidize it because it would be much more likely to produce development than the current two-track system.

The second proposal (in Appendix B) has the disadvantage of being more radical but does even more to promote good management and does not necessarily require the reform of the national public service salary system. It builds on the model of the French grand corps, where the salary of higher civil servants is fixed by their standing in their corps rather than their specific job, and where employees are easily "detached" to serve in a variety of positions. The proposal would establish Africa-wide self-governing corps for each of the professions associated with public service. Civil servants of distinction would be elected into these corps, be given a higher salary level through it but remain in their previous local positions, as long as they enjoyed the confidence of their national superiors. Should they be forced out of their local position (or demoted), they would be assisted in finding a position outside the national government, with the corps again guaranteeing their topped-up salary. They could return to national government service at any time, again without prejudice as to their income. Such a system would provide incentives for performance at international levels, encourage professional ties and standards between peers across Africa, encourage integrity, and protect risk takers. It also would ensure that governmental and nongovernmental organizations had a supply of strong local professionals upon whom they could draw, permitting them to choose talented managers whose values and priorities were responsive to their policy objectives. This option helps to strengthen almost all the components of managerial performance, but it has the disadvantage of requiring sustained finance from international development agencies. It also does not address problems at the junior staff level, although it does provide incentives for upwardly mobile middle managers. Thus this option is best thought of as a system that creates a cadre of outstanding top managers and policymakers, even in countries that are too weak to adopt the first, public service commission, option. The two models actually would interact with and reinforce each other quite well.

To further thinking about these alternatives, it might be helpful to have research done on the ways in which multinational businesses and international NGOs have handled these issues. They face a similarly bifurcated labor market, but they have much greater flexibility in dealing with it. Of course, they have one substantial advantage over donors trying to work through national governments—there is no question that the employees' long-term interests are best served by attending to the interests of their employer and that these interests are appropriate. In the case of African civil servants working on donor projects, employees may choose to emphasize the interests of either the donor or of their political head, and the two sets of interests may well not only diverge substantially from one another but appeal to conflicting systems of legitimacy. The proposals advanced above seek to mitigate that problem by creating incentives for good performance while facilitating the movement of managers and other professionals to those organizations where their values are best aligned with and most responsive to those in charge.

The approach advocated here is a radical one, but radical in the original sense of that word—that it goes to the very roots of the problem. Given the magnitude of the present crisis, we do not believe that anything else will suffice.

Next Steps

The nature of the capacity-building problem facing Africa today is very different from the one encountered at independence. In the 1960s, incentives for public service were strong, and functional organizations in which to learn informally on the job were in place. The need then was for more managers with strong formal training. Today, formal qualifications are much less of a problem.

The most urgent need today is to find ways to redress the inadequate incentives for effective performance being offered to African development managers. This is not just an issue of pay and retention; it is a matter of motivating the learning and application of appropriate skills. The ad hoc measures currently being used do not meet the defining criteria for an adequate incentive system, which would provide

1. a potentially sustainable way
2. to reward and retain outstanding local managers and
3. to expand the pool of local managerial talent
4. without simply adding to the pool of resources that are corruptly traded within the system.

Once the incentive structure surrounding African development management has been remedied, it is possible to think of other measures that would enhance capacity as well. They include efforts to build development-related professions through training programs and international professional contacts and to enhance the training of the most senior African public servants so as to nurture their own staff in the tacit learning of good management on the job.

There is no presumption in these proposals that professionalism alone can rescue Africa from the serious problems of public policy and administration into which it has fallen all too frequently. All one can hope for is the creation of "pockets of excellence" within the civil service that can provide good service within their own domains, grow as conditions permit, and serve as an example to the rest of the government of what is possible. There is substantial evidence that national civil services need not be uniformly good or bad. Even states with quite dismal standards in most of their public services frequently have exceptional units that exhibit high performance. These pockets of productivity become the growth points for positive change when political and social conditions are favorable.[25] We need to create and sustain them to provide for the future of African development.

4

The Causes of Civil
Conflict in Africa

IN PUBLIC AND ACADEMIC DEBATES, AFRICA IS TOO OFTEN DISMISSED AS A continent of violence and chaos. As we stated at the outset of this book, this image of barbarous Africa is exaggerated, misleading, and sometimes racist. However, sub-Saharan Africa is the region with the highest rates of civil conflict on the globe.[1] Some of these conflicts have endured for decades and have been the life experience of more than one generation. This fact—Africa's vulnerability to long, debilitating, and deadly internal wars—must be recognized. Academics have an obligation to understand and explain civil conflict, and policymakers have a responsibility to try to rectify it. In this chapter, we address the first part of this equation, and in the next, David Leonard proposes a practical policy that could break the grip that conflicts currently hold on the continent.

Our approach to explaining Africa's vulnerability to civil conflict builds on the approach we pursued in Chapter 1. We argued there that the dominant paradigm for understanding Africa's multivalent development problems—the personal rule framework—was not wrong. Rather, we emphasized that efforts to understand Africa's development problems should not stop with personal rule but also explore what underlies its persistence. To that end, we underlined Africa's colonial legacy of weak states and its current dependence on enclave production and foreign aid. In Chapter 2, we argued that aid dependence and overwhelming indebtedness contribute to these dynamics of personal rule and poor development.

In this chapter, we again start from the public's usual paradigm for understanding Africa's vulnerability to civil conflict—ethnicity. But we will labor to disabuse readers that "tribalism," Africa's high levels of ethnic diversity, or its artificial states are the secret to explaining the continent's high rates of civil conflict. Rather, building on recent work in this field, we again try to shift the analytic orientation to the structural conditions that allow war to be waged. That leads us to focus on how conflict is sustained—on its feasibility. In so doing, we will return to our themes of enclave production and weak states, showing that they can lead not only to personal rule and poor development but also to civil war and rebellion as well.

Ethnicity and Civil Conflict

Almost all civil conflict in Africa is enmeshed in local politics. The key actors who prosecute civil conflicts all fight for something, whether that goal be political power, control of lucrative economic markets, or defeat of a rival. To gain legitimacy for their cause or to win recruits, the elites who promote civil conflict often justify their cause as part of a grander scheme. Fighting in the name of a community is one way to gain support and to situate one's cause in a nobler framework—on behalf of one's own.

Generally speaking, Africa is no different from the rest of the world on this score. The world over, conflict is waged in the name of communities, whether they be nations, religions, ethnic groups, or some combination thereof. In Africa, the most frequent community on behalf of which conflict is waged is an ethnic one. There are various reasons for this situation. The most important is that modern African politics is rooted in the continent's colonial experience, and colonialism was organized around logics of race and ethnicity. In other words, colonialism was predicated on Europeans' racial supremacy, and its local applications in Africa were organized around and through the supposed "tribes" they found there, a point that will be developed below.

Not recognizing the importance of ethnicity in Africa is intellectually dishonest. But recognizing ethnicity's salience is not equivalent to explaining why sub-Saharan Africa is so vulnerable to civil conflict. Even though conflicts may be waged in the name of an ethnic community, or one perceived to be ethnic, the persistence and prevalence of civil conflict may have to do with other factors. Since this point is so fundamental, we want to focus on it more explicitly.

In nonacademic and even some academic circles, if one asks why there is so much civil conflict in Africa, the most common answer is "tribalism." Civil conflict is here seen as an "ancient" way of being: tribes are said to have been fighting each other for millennia. In this perspective, civil conflict is either irrational or so ingrained as to defy explanation and amelioration. When applied to Africa, sometimes this mode of argument is racist: Africans are portrayed as constitutionally prone to irrationality. At other times, the claim reflects a lack of careful thinking; the assumption is that Africans are fighting today because they always have been fighting.

This type of argument has been refuted many times, but given its prevalence, at least in nonacademic circles, it bears refutation once more.[2] The racist argument is simply wrong (and offensive). Africans are not any more or less irrational than any other regional grouping. And the concept of race itself is bogus when applied to large social groupings. As for the more complex version of the tribalism argument—what is called "primordialism" because conflicts are said to be "age-old" and are presented as not being connected to contemporary social and political contexts—it also is empirically untenable. Ethnic groupings in Africa are modern constructions, often engendered under colonialism. Almost no contemporary conflicts correspond to ones found in precolonial times.[3] Only 10 percent of Africa's states have contemporary ethnic conflicts that are traceable to the preindependence era, and most often they are evidence of the changes caused by the introduction of the *colonial* state.[4] In fact, colonialism sometimes created ethnic groups where they previously did not exist, and at the least substantially changed the terms by which communities defined themselves in public arenas.[5]

Recognizing that ethnic conflict is not "natural" has been a starting point for two other schools of thought on ethnic conflict. These approaches are variously and sometimes interchangeably labeled "constructivist" and "instrumentalist."[6] "Constructivism" recognizes that ethnic groups and ethnic identity are socially constructed, that is, ethnic groups are created in specific historical contexts. Constructivism holds that individuals may believe they are members of a group but that this position is not fixed. Individuals' group membership may change over time; individuals belong to several communities at once; and the definition of groups is malleable. Which group a person identifies with and how the group is defined are functions of society and history.

In an African context, the constructivist position is particularly relevant because colonialism introduced new terms and new institutions that changed the way in which Africans constructed their various group memberships. In some cases, clan, status, and lineage affiliations became "ethnic" or "tribal." In other cases, the colonial administrators invented entirely new groups (usually inadvertently). But in both cases, the terms by which groups were defined changed, and colonial states institutionalized these new group formations. Again, emphasizing a colonial legacy demonstrates that "ethnic conflict" is not "ancient" or "time-honored" but modern and historical.

The "instrumentalist" thesis is similar to a constructivist position, with the difference that an instrumentalist position emphasizes that conflict is generated from a top-down struggle for power and resources. A conflict is instrumental because the principal players seek material goods, generally in rational ways; they do so by appealing to ethnic group membership. Ethnicity is here a tool, or instrument, that elites use to leverage their interests. Appealing to group honor thus might be a way to mobilize masses, but the reasons behind that appeal have to do with a desire to gain access to resources, not premodern irrational behavior.[7] As elite interests shift, so too do the ethnic group's boundaries *and* the nature of its adversaries. Here again, ethnicity is recognized as socially constructed, contextual, and politically mobilized. The emphasis is on competition for resources, a process that in Africa was spawned by modernization under colonialism and sustained by postindependence development.[8] The continent offers numerous examples of this type of violence, where elites try to mobilize masses to gain access to newly introduced resources—in particular, the state, which is the primary means in Africa for gaining access to and distributing goods.

In the constructivist or instrumentalist views, Africa's vulnerability to ethnic conflict can be explained in at least three ways. First, the colonial experience was predicated on ruling through ethnic groups and on seeing "tribe" as the central social unit in Africa. As such, both the institutions Africa inherited and the terms by which Africans recognized political communities emphasized ethnic groups. Second, the colonial experience created state borders that did not previously exist and that included, in some cases, huge numbers of ethnic groups (some 200 in the case of the Democratic Republic of Congo, for example). Africa would be vulnerable, then, to conflict because of its artificial and irrationally created colonial borders. And third, in the same vein, colonial borders often encompassed groups that previously were in conflict or that had little culturally to do with one another.

An assumption underlying these last two points is that where states and nations do not correspond, conflict ensues. Africa's colonial expe-

[handwritten margin notes: "actors", "screw you without cultural gift giving."]

rience made "ethnic groups" and "tribes" the primary basis of group identification. As such, when independence was granted, these states were nations only in name. States were conglomerations of ethnic groups whose members saw their group as more salient than a common, multiethnic "national" entity. This fact, coupled with low levels of economic development, made Africa vulnerable to conflict: to cite a common metaphor, with a small "state cake" to slice into many parts, Africa was vulnerable to conflict.

This argument is plausible only up to a point. One test would be whether levels of ethnic diversity might correlate with levels of conflict, but that is not the case. Somalia, which has one ethnic group, and Rwanda and Burundi, which supposedly have three (even though Hutu, Tutsi, and Twa speak one language and do not possess other common attributes of ethnic groups), have recently experienced some of the world's most intense civil conflicts. Moreover, defining the nature of different groups poses a problem: Does Sudan have two main ethnic groups (blacks and Arabs) or many, since most southern and northern groups (the south is generally considered "black" and the north "Arab") themselves can be divided into smaller ethnic groupings? One more point might be made in this regard: an argument lauding the peacefulness of national communities can rest on a nationalist fiction. Most national communities in the world were artificially constructed at some point in time, and most today are quite multiethnic, even those that at some point were believed to be homogeneous.[9]

Recent large-scale cross-national studies have confirmed that ethnic fractionalization is not the driving cause of conflict.[10] In a series of papers, Paul Collier and his associates at the World Bank have done cross-country analyses of the causes of the civil wars that occurred around the world between 1965 and 1999. Collier and Anke Hoeffler argue that not only is ethnic diversity not a cause of civil conflict but that higher levels of diversity actually decrease the likelihood of domestic conflict.[11] Other cross-national empirical studies from the Bank group support the claim that ethnic diversity does not increase the chances of civil conflict.[12]

Two other sets of scholars beyond Collier's World Bank group have attempted large-sample cross-national analyses of post–World War II incidences of civil conflict. They differ in important but sometimes subtle ways in their methodologies and their conclusions, even though they have built on one another. From the vantage point of this book, however, the importance lies in their agreements, not their disagreements. The first of these efforts is the State Failure Task Force.

The project finds a modest effect for Africa from "the presence of communal groups that are subject to significant economic or political constraints." But the task force also acknowledges that "this result was only weakly statistically significant and should be viewed as suggestive rather than conclusively demonstrated," that other factors are more important, and that the effect is not replicated in its analysis of the full set of world cases.[13] The most recent analysis—and in many ways the most careful and sophisticated of the three—is that of James Fearon and David Laitin of Stanford University. They are even more categorical than Collier that a country's ethnic divisions do not explain the outbreak of civil wars, even if they may be mobilized for their prosecution.[14]

The constructivist and instrumentalist arguments make important advances on understanding civil conflict in Africa. They rightly emphasize that ethnic conflict is not natural or an unchanging essence. This is not to say that ethnicity is not a powerful register for politics in Africa or that ethnic group membership is not highly salient to actors themselves—a point that the constructivist position makes explicit—but rather to say that ethnicity is historical. The arguments also rightly emphasize that conflict is not generated simply by the fact of another group's existence. In other words, Africa's high rates of linguistic and cultural diversity do not explain the continent's high levels of conflict. This is an important point, one that can be forgotten when projecting on the basis of the U.S. experience: in Africa, difference alone is rarely the reason to prosecute violence.

But the instrumentalist and constructivist approaches beg the question as to whether ethnicity itself is key to why conflict occurs in Africa. They suggest that the dynamics driving a conflict may not in fact be about ethnicity itself, even if a conflict is waged in the name of a particular ethnic group. We believe that this point is worth emphasizing: the causes of conflict in Africa need to be separated from ethnicity. Ethnicity *is* a background condition on which conflict can be built, but the forms in which it is present in Africa do not explain the prevalence of civil conflict there. Collier's most recent work does suggest that the dominance of a single ethnic group can promote conflict, but this situation is rarely found in Africa. The continent's ethnic fragmentation again is shown to diminish the prospect of conflict, all other things being equal.[15] Thus the contemporary high rates of conflict in Africa cannot be attributed to the prevalence of multiethnic states.

Enclave Production, Weak States, and Civil Conflict

The understanding of civil conflict needs to be pushed further. Constructivist and instrumentalist accounts still root conflict in the motivations of different cross-sections of society. They portray conflict as generated by a desire for resources on the parts of elites and the symbolic and psychological power for the masses of belonging to a group. Other analyses emphasize "fear" and "security dilemmas" (i.e., "we must kill them before they kill us") as prompting a spiral of violence.[16] Although in any given case these observations might be insightful and valid, recent research pushes the analysis of civil conflict in a different direction. We refine that research and suggest it offers more purchase, at an aggregate level, than the two approaches already discussed when it comes to explaining why sub-Saharan Africa is particularly vulnerable to civil conflict.

We start from the theoretical proposition that elites seek to gain access to resources and that they want to mobilize as many people as they can to achieve that end. Ethnicity may matter in determining the shape of a particular conflict—in terms of who is considered an enemy, who is considered a friend, and how violence is carried out—but ethnicity itself is not the cause of a conflict's start or persistence. Furthermore, there may be a large range of possible motivations for why individuals adhere to one side of a conflict and would want to mobilize. They could include fear or greed, a desire to settle scores or protect one's family, or even hatred. Assuming these points, we ask, What are the conditions that allow civil conflict to persist? And in the African context, we want to explore, at an aggregate level, whether African economies have features that make them particularly vulnerable to sustained civil conflict.

The starting point for this discussion is the recent work of Paul Collier and his associates at the World Bank. Collier argues that warring actors' stated reasons for civil conflict do not hold the key to understanding why a conflict occurs. In other words, even if rebel leaders say they are fighting because of inequality, discrimination, authoritarianism, or other "grievances," they are not the enabling causes of conflict. Rather, since grievance is widespread in society[17] and rebels and those who only protest make similar demands, Collier argues that

> it is the feasibility of predation which determines the risk of conflict. Predation may be just a regrettable necessity on the road to perceived

justice or power, but it is the conditions for predation which are decisive. Whether conflict is motivated by predation, or simply made
possible by it, these two accounts come to the same conclusion:
rebellion is unrelated to objective circumstances of grievance while
being caused by the feasibility of predation.[18]

We will explore this argument in detail. But first it should be noted
that "feasibility of predation" is not a monocausal variable for Collier
and his colleagues. Collier and Hoeffler argue that slow economic
growth and low national income limit the resources with which governments can deter rebellions.[19] Africa's poor economic performance
since the 1980s therefore partly explains why the continent has witnessed a recent upsurge in conflict. Collier also contends that "geography matters," meaning that the more dispersed a population, the more
likely a rebellion will take place,[20] and finally that "history matters,"
meaning that the risks of conflict are greater if a country has recently
experienced some violence.[21] In fact, Collier has found that in the first
decade after peace has been restored, civil conflict has double the
chance of recurring than it had of breaking out in the first place.[22]
But the key insight in the Collier argument rests on the feasibility
of predation. This approach follows from seeing rebellions as organizations that need to finance themselves. The world has any number of
organizations that would attach societal resources to pursue their interests if they could—Collier calls rebel predation "illegal taxation."[23] But
some economies are more vulnerable to predation than others, according to Collier. In particular, an economy that is dependent on the export
of primary products is vulnerable to predation, which translates into a
higher risk for conflict. Primary product exports are easily comman-
deered because they have asset specificity and because their transportation creates opportunities, or "choke points," where they can be
looted.[24] Primary product exports are, in short, "lootable and taxable."
When one-third of a country's GNP is made up of mineral and agricultural exports, the risks of civil conflict are at their peak.[25] Africa, then,
is particularly vulnerable to civil conflict because of the continent's
overwhelming economic dependence on the international sale of primary products.
The World Bank group approach to civil conflict has much to com-
mend it. The economic approach to civil conflict is particularly insightful in explaining how civil conflicts can be sustained. A range of circumstances might exist for why a conflict starts, but focusing on the

means by which rebel organizations finance themselves helps answer why conflicts can persist for long periods of time. Indeed, in the African context, some wars have lasted for decades—in Angola, in particular. The World Bank group economic approach helps us see that the persistence of these conflicts has little to do with grievance or ethnicity. Rather, these conflicts start and last because the economic structures provide rebel organizations with the means by which to continue to survive and sometimes do well out of war.

To be sure, not every question that relates to civil conflict is answered in this formulation. In particular, Collier's analysis does not explain why the leaders of an organization would choose rebellion. For Collier, the key to rebellion is the organization's ability to be financially viable, but this view already assumes the existence of a rebel organization. In other words, where the rebel organization comes from is still an important question. Nor does the Collier approach explain *when* conflicts erupt or when they end (assuming that the structure of the economy persists). In all likelihood, local politics—shifting alliances, particular triggers, or sometimes external intervention—will determine the timing of a conflict's onset and its closure. It also seems likely that grievances intensify violence as well as contribute to who is considered an enemy. But overall, in our view, Collier's economic insights represent an outstanding advance for understanding the causes of civil conflict and in particular for understanding a given country's risk for protracted conflict.

At the same time, the World Bank group's analysis can be extended. The analysis primarily pertains to the conditions by which rebel organizations can survive. However, it tells only one side of the story. To understand why civil conflicts persist, it also is important to isolate the conditions that permit states to participate in civil conflict. As argued in Chapter 1, the structure of production and the weakness of states in Africa are key.

Collier's concept of "primary product exports" can be further refined. In particular, dependence on enclave production better explains the dynamics that Collier and the other analysts in the World Bank group are analyzing. First, the key aspect of enclave production is that in these circumstances, the ability to wage war is disconnected from the overall productivity of society. Even in the midst of economic and state collapse, enclaves continue to produce revenue, which in turn finances conflict. Thus, for both rebels and governments, social destruction caused directly or indirectly by war does not affect the ability to wage it.

One crucial distinction to draw between enclave and primary product production is the dispersion of productivity. Long-standing conflicts inevitably take a toll on society. If a rebel group's or government's revenue depends on the overall economic productivity of a population, then over time, the social costs of war decrease the feasibility of its prosecution. That proposition holds in states that depend on the export of smallholder primary products. This is not the case in enclave economies, where production and revenue are disconnected from the mass of society. In these cases, social and economic deterioration does not limit the feasibility of waging war. Conflicts can last longer with enclave production, and they are unlikely to be sustained without it.

Second, one of the pivots of Collier's analysis of conflict is the feasibility of predation. As argued in Chapter 1, predation can have a short time horizon in economies in which smallholder agricultural production is the predominant source of cash revenues. Smallholders are likely to switch crops if their products are looted or taxed to the point of not providing sufficient returns. Too much predation then jeopardizes the revenue source of both rebel organizations and states. By contrast, enclaves have high asset specificity, making predation sustainable over the long run. Equally, most enclave products—diamonds, gold, oil, and so on—are high-value goods that can be funneled quickly to international markets with fairly limited (in terms of its extent) physical infrastructure. Many enclave products also are easily cashed, requiring minimal financial infrastructure.

The key to emphasize here is that the peculiarities of African economies make the continent structurally vulnerable to civil conflict. Lucrative, geographically confined production that remains aloof from domestic markets is the predominant source of hard currency for many African states. These resources are vulnerable to predation and to protracted conflict. Both rebels and governments can control them, and both can wage war without jeopardizing their principal revenue source. If, in the course of conflict, the wider domestic economy goes to ruin, that collapse would not end the ability to prosecute conflict. In other words, enclave or "rentier" production increases the risk of conflict and especially the chances that conflict can be sustained over long periods of time. Where elites subsist on the collection of taxes and bribes from key, geographically confined production without making much of a productive contribution in return (i.e., when we have a rentier state), countries are vulnerable to conflict. This is a legacy of Africa's contemporary place in the global economy, and it suggests that broader-based, more diversified economies would go a long way toward reducing Africa's risk of conflict. This argument and a policy proposal on how to get there are developed in the next chapter.

Before turning to case studies that illustrate the argument we are making, it is worth pointing out that other revenue sources have similar effects, in terms of vulnerability to civil conflict. In particular, revenues that flow to elites but are disconnected from the general productivity of a population and do not directly contribute to a society's productive capacity can have similar effects as enclaves do. More specifically, remittances from emigrants overseas (diasporas) and foreign aid also contribute to the sustainability of waging war. Again, the financial, organizational costs of violence are offset by revenue streams that are not rooted in the economy where the civil conflict is taking place. Thus, the particularities of Africa's aid-dependent states contribute to their vulnerability to conflict, making international recognition a prize worth fighting for. Diasporic remittances also affect the ability to sustain civil conflict, and a rebel group may be able to tap this resource even in the early stages of its war on the state.[26]

Africa's weak states contribute to the continent's general vulnerability to conflict as well.[27] This condition primarily derives from the institutional legacies of colonialism, the structure of most states' revenue sources, and the concomitant lack of imperatives to gain broad-based legitimacy. But here the point is that weak states inhibit governments' capacity to fight and defeat rebellions. The cash needs of a rebel organization are much less when squaring off against weak states than when facing strong ones. Thus, weak states increase the risk and duration of civil conflicts because governments are less effective in defeating rebellions.[28]

Enclave production and weak states reinforce each other: enclave production lends itself to personal rule, which in turn interacts with weak states. So too do enclave production and weak states reinforce each other at the level of civil conflict. Enclave production positively increases the feasibility of waging war; weak states have less ability to deploy coercive instruments to end conflict.

The argument we are advancing here for the role of enclave export production in African civil conflicts is a variant on the one made by Collier and his associates about dependence on the export of primary products. As such, it requires validation. Unfortunately, the statistics necessary to do a definitive quantitative analysis on enclave production simply do not exist, as we noted in Chapter 1. A qualitative analysis, supplemented by a first approximation of a statistical one, will strengthen our case, however. First we present the qualitative analysis, in which we analyze countries with and without civil conflict in Africa and we discuss the extent to which enclave production has contributed to the outcome.[29] The following sampling of cases indicates both the power of the enclave argument and the fact that it does not explain *all* contingencies.

Enclave Economies with Civil Conflict

Enclave production entails the export of primary products (usually extractive) that are generated in a small area. In Africa, the prevalent forms of enclave production are mining, oil drilling, felling virgin timber, and agricultural production on the estates of large corporations. The enclave idea implies that production is geographically concentrated, that a large portion of the land or capital goods involved in export production cannot easily be assigned to other profitable purposes, and that labor (which always is mobile) is a small part of the cost of production.

Angola is a clear case in which enclave production allowed conflicts to be sustained for long periods of time. Civil war was waged in Angola almost continuously since the country attained independence from Portugal in 1975. The two principal actors in the conflict were the People's Movement for the Liberation of Angola (MPLA), which forms the government in Luanda, and the National Union for the Total Independence of Angola (UNITA), a rebel group based in the northeast. In its early years, Angola had a diversified economy. But discovery of large oil deposits and the continued civil war concentrated government revenue on petroleum products. Today, Angola is sub-Saharan Africa's second-largest oil producer; the country pumps about 740,000 barrels per day, which, together with other petroleum products, amounts to 95 percent of the government's export receipts.[30] Though other oil fields are in the process of being developed, Angolan oil production is concentrated in the Atlantic Ocean enclave of Cabinda, in the country's northwest. The country also has generated substantial revenue from diamonds. Angola is today estimated to be the world's fourth-largest diamond exporter in terms of value. During the Cold War, UNITA largely depended on support from South Africa's apartheid government and from the United States, which saw UNITA as a counterbalance to the socialist MPLA. However, as Cold War and apartheid monies dried up, UNITA succeeded in gaining control of the diamond mines in the Cuango Valley. By one estimate, UNITA raised more than $3.7 billion in this way from 1992 to 1998.[31] Angola represents a classic case of the dangers of enclave dependency. The country overall has collapsed, untold lives have been lost, and corruption is rampant. But high-value enclave products allowed a war to be sustained for more than twenty-five years. Its apparent end has come only after the death of UNITA's leader.[32]

Between 1965 and 1997, the Democratic Republic of Congo (formerly Zaire) was ruled by Mobutu Sese Seko, one of Africa's most colorful and profligate dictators. Covering a large expanse in the center of Africa, the Democratic Republic of Congo is endowed with diamonds, gold, cobalt, copper, zinc, coltan, and virgin timber resources—all enclaves—in addition to fertile agricultural areas in the east. The Democratic Republic of Congo is the world's third-largest producer of diamonds by volume and fifth by value; diamonds account for 64 percent of government export revenue, according to the Economist Intelligence Unit (EIU). By one estimate, they totaled $715 million annually.[33] During his three decades in power, Mobutu relied extensively on "rents" collected from the country's enclaves while reinvesting little in the country's infrastructure. Over time, the state was effectively hollowed out, and Mobutu's regime became the basis for coining the term "kleptocracy."[34] By 1995, according to the EIU, the average Congolese was 53 percent poorer than thirty years previously.

Since 1996, the country has witnessed two multinational wars whose immediate origins stem from its eastern neighbors, Rwanda and Uganda. However, in 2002, the country was divided into several territories, each supported by enclaves. The government controlled the key diamond mines in Kasai, copper and cobalt mines in Katanga, and timber reserves in several provinces, which it seemingly contracted out to its main military backer—Zimbabwe.[35] On the rebel side, Ugandan-backed rebels controlled diamond-, coltan-, and gold-producing areas as well as timber and minor coffee estate holdings in Equateur. Rwandan-backed rebels controlled diamond-, gold-, cassiterite-, and coltan-producing areas.[36] Enclaves clearly contributed to an extreme example of personal rule in the Democratic Republic of Congo and were the foundation for that country's seemingly intractable and multifaceted conflict.[37]

Sierra Leone is another tragic case of entrenched civil conflict that persisted because of enclave production. From 1991, when Liberianbacked rebels of the Revolutionary United Front (RUF) invaded Sierra Leone, until early 2002, that country was at war. Like Angola and the Democratic Republic of Congo, Sierra Leone's cash economy is heavily dependent on high-value mineral exports, in particular alluvial diamonds, which are concentrated in the Kenema, Kono, and Bo districts. The country also has gold, bauxite, and rutile deposits. Mineral exports, of which diamonds were the lion's share, amounted to 80 percent of all export revenue in 1989. The RUF controlled the key diamond-producing area around Kono. A United Nations panel reported that estimates of the value of RUF diamond exports ranged between $25 million and $125 million annually; this amount was said to be "a major and primary source of income for the RUF, and is more than enough to sustain its military activities."[38] In addition to the mineral enclaves the government controls, the state became extremely dependent on foreign aid. The most recent EIU report at the time of writing estimates that Sierra Leone received $232 million from various donors, but the government's exports only amounted to $41.3 million. That report concluded: "The insurgency has resulted in the country's near-total dependence on foreign aid."[39] In short, diamonds and foreign aid clearly permitted the war in Sierra Leone to be sustained.[40] Only British intervention in the country has restored some element of stability.

The West African country of Liberia is also enclave-dependent and was wracked by civil conflict during the 1990s. A six-year factional civil war ended in 1997 with the election of Charles Taylor, a former rebel, though sporadic armed incursions continue. The main enclaves in Liberia have historically been the Firestone rubber plantations, iron ore mines, and timber; the country also has deposits of gold and diamonds. In recent years, the latter has become a lucrative commodity in the country, as Liberia served as an exporter of Sierra Leone's diamonds. A UN Panel of Experts found that although Liberia's domestic capacity for diamond production was roughly 150,000 carats, Belgium reported receiving 2.56 million carats of Liberian origin in 1998, valued at $217 million.[41] In terms of timber, Global Witness estimated Liberia's timber profits at $50–70 million in 1999.[42] However, statistics on Liberia's economy vary considerably. In 1999 the EIU estimated exports at $32 million in rubber, $22 million in timber, and nothing in iron ore, whereas in 1998 the respective figures were $107 million, $94 million, and $208 million. The World Bank does not list Liberia in its comprehensive statistical survey, the *World Development Report*. Nonetheless, the Liberian economy is clearly dependent on enclaves, which has contributed to its vulnerability to sustained civil conflict.

Nigeria also is an enclave-dependent country with a history of civil conflict and extensive corruption. Today it is sub-Saharan Africa's top oil producer. Nigeria produces more than 2 million barrels of oil per day, and oil revenue accounts for 95 percent of the country's export earnings. Oil production started in 1958 and then accelerated in the 1960s and 1970s. Severe ethnic riots preceded the Nigerian civil war of 1967–1970. But one of the factors that led the Igbo to attempt the Biafran secession (and the northern-dominated government to resist it) was the concentration of petroleum deposits in their part of the country.[43]

Without going into detail about the case, we would point out that Congo-Brazzaville (the Republic of Congo) also is an enclave economy with a history of sustained civil conflict. Oil production in that country accounted for some 91 percent of its exports in 1999. The clashes between Bernard Lissouba and Denis Sassou-Nguesso over who would be president clearly were driven by a desire to control this resource.[44]

Mozambique confirms our argument about enclave production in a particularly interesting way. The economy is *not* an enclave one; the country is extremely poor and the forms of production that remained after the Portuguese fled at independence are generally those of small-holder peasants and fishermen (prawns, cashews, and cotton are its primary exports). There are no significant minerals. Nonetheless there was a long postindependence civil war between the Communist-backed Front for the Liberation of Mozambique (FRELIMO) government and a particularly unsavory group of rebels—Mozambique National Resistance (RENAMO)—financed first by white supremacist Rhodesia and then South Africa. In this sense, the rebellion was *not* prosecuted with resources raised from Mozambique's domestic economy but with external subsidies instead. The international system was surprised at how easily a settlement was made between FRELIMO and RENAMO, once the collapse of the Soviet Union deprived the former of military aid and the end of apartheid in South Africa ended the latter's finances. Without either external finance or enclave production, Mozambique could not produce the resources to continue prosecuting a civil war. Negotiations led to UN-supervised multiparty elections and modest demobilization benefits for the guerrillas, who then simply went home.[45]

Somalia also conforms to our thesis in an unorthodox manner. The country's livestock and agricultural production is overwhelmingly performed by smallholders and is quite dispersed. The prosperity of the Gulf oil states added two new enclavelike dimensions to the Somali economy, however. First, large numbers of Somali men emigrated to the Saudi peninsula to work. The greatly overvalued Somali currency made it unattractive to remit these earnings through official channels. As a result, informal bankers, whom the men could trust because of clan ties, became suddenly wealthy and thereby able to finance rebellions. At the same time, the high price being offered for Somali livestock in the Gulf made the Somali ports extremely valuable enclaves. Informal banking wealth combined with the newly valuable target of enclave ports to create and sustain civil war—leading to the overthrow of President Siad Barre and the disintegration of the state into warring fiefdoms. The ports have remained valuable despite the war because most of the livestock that passes through them are raised in surrounding countries. Thus it has been hard to reunify the country or find lasting peace.[46]

Nonenclave Economies Without Civil Conflict

Kenya, Ghana, Tanzania, and Malawi are all examples of countries whose wealth is largely based on peasant production of beverage tree crops—coffee, tea, and cocoa. Each country has seen dramatic tensions around ethnicity, but these grievances have not erupted into major conflicts. There have been ethnic clashes in some of these countries, but with the absence of enclaves on which to prey, there has been no money for rebellions. In Kenya, Kikuyu ethnic complaints against the government of President Daniel arap Moi are particularly strong, and the absence of sustained civil strife there would be surprising if ethnicity or grievance were the key to violent conflict. The fact that its broad-based tourist, tea, and coffee industries—on which the economy depends—all would be destroyed by civil war seems to be a major factor in the calculations of the opposition to use peaceful means of protest. Ghana does have significant gold production, but its overall proportion to foreign exports led us to classify this country as a non–enclave dependent state (gold accounted for 37 percent of foreign exports in 1999). Tanzania similarly has an important mineral production sector (28 percent of foreign exports in 1999), but not enough to qualify as an enclave economy. Malawi is another country largely dependent on smallholder agricultural production and lacking a history of civil conflict.

As we noted in Chapter 1, Senegal has a peasant-based economy. It has experienced some disorder from separatists in the Casamance, which is physically separated from the rest of the country by Gambia. The conflict has stayed low-key, however, which probably is due to the absence of enclave resources. Only a marginal portion of Senegal's overall foreign exports comes from enclaves (phosphates and fertilizers accounted for 13 percent of exports), with the remainder primarily coming from fish, fish products, and groundnuts. Though neighboring Mali has increased its production of gold in recent years (to 41 percent of exports in 1999), that country primarily derives its wealth from peasant production of cotton and has been at peace. Similarly, civil conflict has not afflicted Gambia, Benin, or Togo, all comparatively small countries without significant enclave production—though it should be noted that Togo has had a history of instability in the form of coups and has an important phosphate production sector (26 percent of exports).

Nonenclave Economies with Civil Conflict

Nevertheless, not all smallholder economies escape civil war. Uganda's wealth was in peasant coffee and cotton production, but the misfortune of a coup by the particularly vicious Idi Amin took the country through years of conflict. Similarly, Ethiopia tried to absorb Eritrea and has experienced long years of civil and international war as a result, despite the peasant base of both economies. It is worth noting, though, that the Eritrean independence movement was largely sustained through diasporic funding. *[enclave esc "]*

The analysis of civil conflict presented here also does not apply to cases of genocide and large-scale mass murder. In the African context, the relevant region is the Great Lakes. In Burundi, facing a purported rebellion, Tutsi leaders organized massacres of as many as 200,000 (mostly elite) Hutu in 1972. Burundi also had other periods of extreme violence, notably in 1989 and 1993, and in 2002 was locked in a seemingly intractable, factional civil conflict between the Tutsi-dominated military and government and various Hutu factions. In Rwanda, a Hutu elite launched a genocide in 1994 that resulted in one of the world's worst atrocities.[47] The politics of these two countries does not exclude the possibility of mass violence recurring and the urgent need for international intervention.

The causes of these Great Lakes conflicts are significantly different from the modal type of conflict on the continent. Both states receive large amounts of rents in the form of foreign aid, and in Rwanda's case, conflict in the 1990s was initiated by the Rwandan Patriotic Front—a largely Tutsi movement that depended on funding from its diaspora and from Uganda. However, enclave production and weak states do not structure the Great Lakes conflicts. In these countries, states are dense, covering relatively small territories. Revenue generation primarily derives from smallholder production—much of it coffee—and is spread out across the country. Each conflict is also underpinned by racial ideologies and fears of extermination on both sides, conditions that again are rare on the continent.

The bases of conflict in the Great Lakes create a character of violence that is different from civil conflict in other territories. Today, both governments (notably Rwanda) are involved in a multinational conflict in the Democratic Republic of Congo, a conflict that is very much sustained by enclave production. However, Great Lakes civil conflict generally takes the form of intense massacres against civilians, with the potential for genocide or large-scale murder. This type of mass violence is rare on the continent, and Africa is no more likely than other regions of the world to be the arena for it.

Sudan and Chad also have long-standing conflicts but to date have not been enclave-dependent. However, both countries' economic structures are changing to become oil-based. Sudan and Chad are large territories marked by a decisive division between north and south; this division is overlaid with an apparent ethnic and religious division (particularly in Sudan) between Arab Muslims in the north and black Christians and animists in the south. In Sudan's case, the south is today overwhelmingly dependent on foreign aid, which makes it the functional equivalent of an enclave. The long-standing civil conflict in Sudan has taken place almost entirely in the south, without substantial disruption in the north. In both countries, violence historically was not financed through enclave production, but in Sudan the prospect of oil production was one factor in leading the southern rebels to restart the civil war in 1983 after several years of peace—and the north to resist the secession. These dimensions would lead us to classify Sudan as having an economy that operates as a functional equivalent of an enclave.

Enclave Economies Without Civil Conflict

Just as not all African countries that depend on smallholder agriculture for export income are at peace, so not all mineral-producing countries have seen civil conflict. Botswana, Cameroon, and Gabon all fit in this exceptional category. Three of them are "exceptions that prove the rule." France has made it clear repeatedly that it will intervene militarily to prevent disorder in Cameroon and Gabon, on which it depends for oil.[48] Rebels will never be able to prey on these enclaves—and therefore they are not tempted to try. Similarly, the fact that Botswana borders a South Africa that has been quick to send in troops when disorder threatens makes conflict there unattractive—although the good leadership of Presidents Seretse Khama and Ketumile Matsire deserves even more credit for its peace.

Quantitative Analysis

The pattern of association in Africa between enclave export production and civil conflict is not perfect. Nonetheless, it appears to be quite strong. The data available for measuring the enclave character of African economies are imperfect; statistics on the degree to which agricultural production is concentrated on estates are particularly elusive. Nonetheless, we have been able to come close.

In Table 4.1, we present data on those thirty-seven sub-Saharan African countries that had achieved majority rule before 1990 (i.e., Eritrea, Namibia, and South Africa are excluded). We use the World Bank group's listing of conflicts—those in which there were at least 1,000 fatalities in a single year—save for those that were wars of independence from colonialism, which we believe have different causal dynamics.[49] (This decision excludes Guinea-Bissau, as well as Eritrea, Namibia, and South Africa. The wars of independence in Angola and Mozambique are excluded by this criterion as well, but both had civil wars after independence.)

To construct an indicator of an enclave economy, in Table 4.1 we provide several statistics for 1999—the GNP of each country; the value of its exports; exports as a percentage of GNP; the value of exports from minerals, timber, and enclave agriculture; the percentage of exports that these three forms of enclave production make up; and the

Table 4.1   World Bank Group Conflicts and Enclave Production in Sub-Saharan Africa

Country	Postindependence Conflict	Enclave	GNP[a] (millions $)	Exports[b] (millions $)	Exports as a % of GNP	Value of Exports from			Enclave as % of Exports	Enclave as % of GNP
						Minerals[c] (millions $)	Timber (millions $)	Enclave Agriculture (millions $)		
Angola	yes	yes	5,606	4,970	88.7	4,892			98	87
Benin	no	no	2,300	422	18.3				0	0
Botswana	no	yes	5,100	2,671	52.4	2,220			83	44
Burkina Faso	no	no	2,600	254	9.8	15			6	1
Burundi	yes	no	800	56	7.0				0	0
Cameroon	no	yes	8,500	1,715	20.2	936	407		78	16
Central African Republic	no	no	1,000	195	19.5	62	48		56	11
Chad	yes	no	1,600	288	18.0				0	0
Congo, Democratic Republic of (Zaire)[d]	yes	yes	5,500	749	13.6	697			93	13
Congo, Republic of (Brazzaville)	yes	yes	1,900	1,668	87.8	1,526	71		96	84
Côte d'Ivoire	no	no	10,400	4,542	43.7	545	273		18	8
Ethiopia	yes	no	6,600	467	7.1				0	0
Gabon	no	yes	4,043	2,394	59.2	1,964	328		96	57
Gambia	no	no	430	121	28.1				0	0
Ghana	no	no	7,400	2,116	28.6	711	174		42	12
Guinea[e]	no	no	3,700	693	18.7	490			71	13
Guinea-Bissau	no	no	195	27	13.8				0	0
Kenya	no	no	10,600	1,741	16.4	100		298	23	4
Lesotho	no	no	1,200	201	16.8				0	0
Liberia[f]	yes	yes	n.a.	43			12	29	95	n.a.
Malawi	no	no	2,000	416	20.8					0
Mali	no	no	2,600	569	21.9	231			41	9
Mauritania	no	no	1,000	333	33.3	130			39	13

continues

Table 4.1 continued

Country	Postindependence Conflict	Enclave	GNP[a] (millions $)	Exports[b] (millions $)	Exports as a % of GNP	Value of Exports from			Enclave as % of Exports	Enclave as % of GNP
						Minerals[c] (millions $)	Timber (millions $)	Enclave Agriculture (millions $)		
Mozambique	yes	no (yes)	3,900	255	6.5	106			0	0
Niger	no	no	2,000	385	19.3				28	5
Nigeria[g]	yes	yes	37,900	20,441	53.9	18,897			92	50
Rwanda[h]	yes	no	2,100	65	3.1				0	0
Senegal[i]	no	no	4,700	1,027	21.9	137			13	3
Sierra Leone[j]	yes	yes	700	43	6.1	37			86	5
Somalia[k]	yes	no (yes)	514	59	11.5				0	0
Sudan	yes	no (yes)	9,435	780	8.3	276			35	3
Swaziland	no	no	1,379	900	65.3	11	97	147	28	18
Tanzania[l]	no	no	8,000	540	6.8	150			28	2
Togo	no	no	1,500	391	26.1	102			26	7
Uganda	yes	no	6,800	n.a.	n.a.				<10	n.a.
Zambia	yes	no	3,200	759	23.7	457			60	14
Zimbabwe	no	no	6,100	2,140	35.1	19		30	2	1

Notes: n.a.: data is not available.
a. World Bank, *World Development Report, 2000/2001,* for 1999 unless otherwise noted. All figures are millions of U.S. dollars.
b. 2001 EIU Country Reports, based on 1999 figures.
c. EIU Country Reports.
d. Based on 2000 GDP figures cited in the 2001 Country Profile Report.
e. Based on 1998 export figures.
f. Based on 1998 export figures.
g. Based on EIU and official estimates of oil exports for 2000.
h. Based on 1998 export figures.
i. Based on 1998 export figures.
j. Based on 1995/1996 export figures (those cited in the Economist Intelligence Unit's Country Profiles).
k. Based on 1998 GDP figures.
l. GNP based on mainland Tanzania.

Table 4.2   Enclave Economies and Civil Conflict

		ENCLAVE?	
		Yes (1)	No (0)
CONFLICT?	Yes (1)	6	8
	No (0)	3	20

Yates $X^2 =$ 2.74 $p < 0.10$

percentage of GNP that enclave exports comprise.[50] We classify as enclave economies those countries in which at least 75 percent of the value of their exports in 1999 was made up of minerals, timber, and estate agriculture. All three of these forms of production are weakly integrated with the general economy, do not depend on the economic productivity of the general population, and are able to operate with limited state infrastructure.

The simple relationship between enclave production and civil conflict is presented in Table 4.2. The pattern found there is statistically significant. Moreover, many of the "deviant cases" in that table are easily explained. If one were to classify Mozambique, Somalia, and Sudan as the functional equivalent of enclave economies, as we have argued they were, the propensity of an enclave economy to be a breeding ground for civil war is even clearer, as is demonstrated by Table 4.3. Even this adjusted table does not take account of the role that French guarantees played in preventing conflict in Cameroon and Gabon nor the similar role that the presence of apartheid South Africa had for Botswana. When all is taken into account, therefore, the case for a relationship between enclave production and civil conflict is quite powerful.

Table 4.3   Enclave Economies and Civil Conflict—Adjusted

		ENCLAVE?	
		Yes (1)	No (0)
CONFLICT?	Yes (1)	9	5
	No (0)	3	20

Yates $X^2 =$ 8.22 $p < 0.005$

The World Bank group's analysis of the causes of civil conflict is not the only one available. Fearon and Laitin of Stanford University have provided an alternative. Although Fearon and Laitin build on the Bank studies, they make minor revisions in the list of conflicts and reach somewhat different conclusions than Collier and his colleagues do.[51] This variation raises the question of whether our findings about the importance of enclaves are robust when they are applied to somewhat different data and another model is used. The simple answer is that our hypotheses emerge even stronger. Part of the Fearon and Laitin explanation for civil conflict is state weakness, which they measure by using GDP per capita. A much better indicator of the capacity of a state to administer its decisions and reach its population is its ability to collect taxes from its citizens.[52] Thus in Table 4.4 we provide data on the percentage of GDP that is collected by a country from purely domestic sources—taxes on goods and services and on income and profits. We exclude income from ODA (aid) and from taxes on exports (which are easy to collect at a port rather than from the producers). Oil companies in particular often are made to pay taxes on corporate income, so our indicator is not a perfect one. But there is no better. We measure domestic tax capacity around 1976 because it shows us the strength of a state before, not after, conflict may have begun. (We also looked at data from the mid-1980s and got nearly the same results.) When there was absolutely no data at all about tax collections in any time period close to 1976, we felt that it was a valid indicator that the state had extremely small penetrative capacity and that it was reasonable to give it a zero score.

We then used multiple regression to see what variables would best explain the number of years of civil conflict a country had had after 1976. The results are presented in Table 4.5. They show that the presence of significant enclave production in a country (as adjusted in Table 4.1 in making the World Bank group's analysis) and the strength of the state (as measured by percentage of GDP collected in domestic taxes) are both highly significant statistically and together account for a quarter of the variance (roughly speaking, variation) in the cases. These are strong findings for error-prone, cross-national analyses of this sort. A country that has an important production enclave on average is found to have had 6.5 more years of civil conflict than one that does not. And for every percentage point increase in GDP collected in domestic taxes, the number of years of civil conflict is decreased by 0.7 years. A simi-

Table 4.4   State Capacity and Fearon and Laitin Years of Conflict

Country	Years of Postinde-pendence Conflict[a] (a)	Adj. Enclave[b] (b)	Domestic Taxes (% of GDP)[c] (c = e+f)	Tax Revenue (% of GDP) (d)	Taxes on Goods and Services (% of GDP) (e)	Taxes on Income, Profits, and Capital Gains (% of GDP) (f)
Angola	25	yes	0.0[d]			
Benin	0	no	4.6	14.2	1.8	2.8
Botswana	0	yes	4.3	12.5	0.1	4.2
Burkina Faso	0	no	3.2	9.1	1.8	1.4
Burundi	2	no	4.2[e]	11.5	2.0	2.2
Cameroon	0	yes	5.3	14.4	2.8	2.5
Central African Republic	2	no	0.0	15.0		
Chad	24	no	2.8	8.8	1.2	1.6
Congo, Democratic Republic of (Zaire)	11	yes	2.9	6.3	0.9	2.0
Congo, Republic of (Brazzaville)	2	yes	10.4	21.5	3.8	6.6
Côte d'Ivoire	0	no	7.9	21.1	5.2	2.7
Ethiopia	21	no	5.8	12.8	3.1	2.7
Gabon	0	yes	10.1	19.9	1.3	8.8
Gambia	0	no	1.6	13.3	0.3	1.3
Ghana	0	no	6.0	11.7	3.3	2.7
Guinea	0	no	0.0			
Guinea-Bissau	3	no	0.0			
Kenya	0	no	10.8	15.7	5.3	5.5
Lesotho	0	no	2.1	16.5	0.7	1.4
Liberia	8	yes	12.3	18.7	4.3	8.0
Malawi	0	no	8.1	11.9	3.3	4.8
Mali	6	no	4.9	10.7	2.5	2.4
Mauritania	0	no	8.9	17.5	5.2	3.7
Mozambique	19	yes	0.0			

continues

lar analysis of the World Bank group data on conflict produces very similar results. Thus these analyses give strong support to the argument that we made in Chapter 1 regarding the importance of enclaves and state weakness to politics, economics, and civil conflict in Africa.

The quantitative analysis we have provided here is a very simple one. To produce a comprehensive picture of the larger causes of civil conflict, the enclave and state weakness variables we have studied here would have to be folded into a larger, much more complex economet-ric model, such as the ones being worked on by Collier and his associ-ates at the World Bank and by Fearon and Laitin at Stanford University. The simple analysis provided here is sufficient for our purposes, how-

Table 4.4   continued

Country	Years of Postinde-pendence Conflict[a] (a)	Adj. Enclave[b] (b)	Domestic Taxes (% of GDP)[c] (c = e+f)	Tax Revenue (% of GDP) (d)	Taxes on Goods and Services (% of GDP) (e)	Taxes on Income, Profits, and Capital Gains (% of GDP) (f)
Niger	0	no	4.7	9.9	2.0	2.7
Nigeria	4	yes	5.1	17.1	2.6	2.5
Rwanda	14	no	3.0	10.3	1.3	1.7
Senegal	3	no	9.1	17.5	4.5	4.6
Sierra Leone	10	yes	5.2	12.2	2.1	3.1
Somalia	20	yes	3.4	10.4	2.6	0.8
Sudan	28	yes	5.8	14.6	4.2	1.6
Swaziland	0	no	8.6	21.1	0.7	7.9
Tanzania	0	no	12.0	17.1	7.3	4.7
Togo	0	no	10.7	22.7	3.3	7.4
Uganda	15	no	3.8	9.0	3.1	0.7
Zambia	0	no	15.5	20.2	8.3	7.2
Zimbabwe	0	no	15.3	19.3	4.3	11.0

Notes: Data are from the most recent world development indicators. Where 1976 data were unavailable, figures were sought for other years between 1974 and 1980. If they were unavailable, estimates for 1981–1990 were accepted from World Bank, *World Development Report 1997: The State in a Changing World* (Washington, D.C.: Oxford University Press, 1997), table A.1.

a. Years of post-1975, postindependence conflict as defined by James D. Fearon and David D. Laitin, "Ethnicity, Insurgency and Civil War," paper presented to the annual meetings of the American Political Science Association, San Francisco, August 30–September 2, 2001. Case list, p. 39.

b. As defined in text.

c. Taxes on international trade were excluded, as were other taxes and nontax revenue.

d. Where no data of any kind on tax revenue were available, a zero was assigned to the case as a valid indicator of its relative state capacity.

e. Apparent discrepancies in addition are due to rounding errors.

ever. It demonstrates that the large and growing presence of enclave economies in Africa, together with weak states, leave the countries of the continent highly vulnerable to rebellions and civil wars.

Conclusion

A clear consensus has developed among scholars that the roots of civil conflict in Africa are structural, not cultural. Ethnicity frequently shapes the boundaries of conflict and often provides an idiom with which to mobilize support and gain legitimacy. However, ethnicity is

Table 4.5   Fearon and Laitin Years of Conflict by Domestic Taxes in Late 1970s as Percentage of GDP and Adjusted Enclave

Regression Statistics	
Multiple R	0.504
R Square	0.255
Adjusted R Square	0.211
Standard Error	7.697
Observations	37

	Coefficients	Standard Error	t Stat	P-value
Intercept	7.750	2.421	3.201	0.003
Domestic Taxes	−0.676	0.304	−2.221	0.033
Adjusted Enclave	6.470	2.713	2.385	0.023

not the driving cause of most conflict; nor are grievances. Rather, the structural feasibility of war is the primary cause. But instead of pointing just to primary products, economic growth, and geography as the structural bases of feasibility, we stress enclave export production and the weak states they help to create. As long as Africa's wealth is based on the export of minerals and agricultural products produced by large corporations in protected enclaves, the continent will be vulnerable to civil war.

The danger created by enclaves and weak states for Africa is neither isolated nor diminishing. As the continent's developmental crisis persists, more governments have become heavily dependent on overseas development assistance, which by separating revenue from the economic productivity of the population frequently operates as the functional equivalent of an enclave. Similarly, private foreign direct investment of capital for diversified production (and a consequent escape from an enclave economy) is frightened away by the frequency of civil conflict on the continent. How is sub-Saharan Africa to escape this vicious circle? One step is the remittance of debt and the reduction of foreign aid that we advocated in Chapter 2. A direct remedy to the security problem itself is the subject of the next chapter.

5

Civil Conflict
and International
Humanitarian Intervention

THE STRONG TENDENCY FOR ENCLAVE EXPORT PRODUCTION TO FOSTER civil conflict creates a vicious circle for Africa. The foreign investments needed for the kinds of development that would move African economies away from their reliance on the export of primary commodities and give them deeper roots in the productive capacities of a broad sweep of the populace are not likely to be made as long as civil conflict remains such an active threat. Just as bad, the continent's weak economic performance has created an unusually great dependence on foreign aid. The large amounts of overseas development assistance available are also predatory targets, which create and sustain civil conflicts and prevent the economic recovery that would lessen dependence on aid. A similar vicious circle exists around the weak capacity of states. Weak states are more vulnerable to civil conflict, and their capacity for dealing with their citizens becomes weaker still as a result of these violent conflicts. If the international system were able to limit the danger of civil conflict in Africa, it would have profound, positive developmental consequences. In particular, given that the chances of conflict increase after an initial outbreak of violence, the most efficient way to deal with civil conflict in Africa is to prevent it from occurring in the first place.

This chapter was researched and written by David K. Leonard.

Humanitarianism and Humanitarian Intervention

In the decade since the Cold War ended, human rights and humanitarianism have moved to center stage in the world of international policy. United Nations Secretary-General Kofi Annan, as well as key Security Council member states, notably the United States, have made human rights and humanitarianism the standard for assessing state behavior and for guiding international action.[1] This attention has prompted a discussion as to whether a new norm of humanitarian military intervention that would trump the norm of sovereignty is emerging.[2]

In the 1990s, Africa experienced various military intervention and peacekeeping missions under a variety of international auspices in the Congo, Eritrea and Ethiopia, Liberia, Sierra Leone, and Somalia. None of these occurred without the consent of the African nation involved, but the embarrassment of the international system at its *failure* to intervene in a timely and effective manner in Rwanda combines with them to put meat on the bones of the sovereignty debate. What shape should humanitarian interventions in Africa take in the twenty-first century so that they both become effective and do not lead to escalating demands in the decades to come?

Because the debate around humanitarian intervention is relatively new, the field's concepts do not have established definitions. For our purposes, "humanitarianism" refers to an international standard protecting the individual rights of citizens of a particular state. In practice, humanitarianism can refer to human rights, such as civil liberties and protection against violence, as well as to more general concerns such as a right to food, water, and health. Humanitarianism is distinguishable from primarily strategic concerns, such as military and economic interests. Intervention here refers to any external action inside a sovereign nation's territory. In this chapter, we are concerned with international military interventions.

Note, however, that the analysis we will offer has only limited application to the genocidal conflicts in Rwanda and Burundi. Although the international responses we outline would apply to preventing mass violence in the Great Lakes, the underlying causes of conflict will not immediately change there—for they are not driven by enclave conditions of economic production. It is also worth noting, though, that these conflicts are ones for which norms of military humanitarian intervention already exist, notably the Convention on the Prevention and Punishment of Genocide. This convention is one of the only international agreements that obligates signatory states to intervene.[3]

International Responses to Civil Conflict in Africa

During the Cold War, unilateral foreign interventions were common in Africa, particularly by France but also the United States and South Africa. The ostensible reason given for these interventions was often humanitarian, but the underlying rationale more often was the mainte- nance of spheres of influence driven by strategic, economic, and diplo- matic interests. (Africa was once thought to be important for the votes it could deliver in the UN General Assembly.) With the Cold War over, Africa seems unlikely to be a venue of significant unilateral interven- tion by the major powers; they lack the interests to do so.[4] Now that France has retreated (although not wholly retired) as hegemon for Fran- cophone Africa, South Africa and Nigeria are the only powers likely to claim the role in Africa south of the Sahara—and recently even they have been cautious to seek regional sanction in doing so.

The position of the collectivity of African states on humanitarian intervention is therefore particularly relevant. As a group, they wel- come the *principle* of humanitarian intervention, especially by regional organizations, but in practice they are extremely delicate about sover- eignty in doing so. They also remain very resistant to the doctrine of national or ethnic self-determination when it is used to argue for a change in existing borders in response to humanitarian crises. The Organization of African Unity (OAU), which unites all the states of the region and is now the African Union (AU), had as its primary organiz- ing principle the inviolability of colonial borders and noninterference with sovereign states. Juridical sovereignty is a matter of passionate concern in Africa precisely because of the fact that empirical statehood is so insecure. Thus neither the OAU/AU nor any significant number of African states have ever sanctioned interventions that threatened national sovereignty. Very few African states supported Biafra in its attempt to secede from Nigeria.

Until very recently, there also has been remarkably little cross-bor- der war in the region and that which has occurred has been tolerated by the African community of states because of its exceptional character. The Tanzanian invasion of Uganda was justified by Idi Amin's prior military foray across the border. The first Rwandan invasion of the

Democratic Republic of the Congo was arguably in "'hot pursuit'" of genocidal militias and was driven by concern with its own security. The Ethiopia-Eritrea war and the second Uganda-Rwanda ventures into the Democratic Republic of the Congo are recent exceptions, and the latter has provoked substantial hostility from other African states.

There are a significant number of regionally sanctioned humanitarian interventions in response to other cases, but all of them came at the request of internationally recognized governments—no matter how slim their claim to empirical sovereignty. Nigeria made significant military interventions in Sierra Leone and Liberia through the Economic Community of West African States (ECOWAS), which has been followed by a UN peacekeeping operation in Sierra Leone.[5] The UN 1960 intervention in the Congo and the present-day involvements there of Angola and Zimbabwe were prompted by the request of the internationally recognized head of state, even if the government's real control over its territory had deteriorated. The multilateral intervention in Somalia occurred under the UN banner, was urged by Secretary-General Boutros Boutros-Ghali (of Egypt), and took place when no internationally recognized government was left.

African leaders tend to feel that the failure of the UN and the rest of the world community to intervene on the continent in the face of genocide or state disintegration is a sign of racist disregard of the lives of Africans, not respect for its territorial integrity. Thus the position of Africa on humanitarian intervention is different from that of other regions of the world. This is not to say that they have no concern for sovereignty—to the contrary, African states were quite critical of the North Atlantic Treaty Organization (NATO) intervention in Kosovo. Where the juridical demands of sovereignty can somehow be fudged, however, African leaders welcome humanitarian interventions by the UN or regional bodies.

Nonetheless, the difficulties of intervention in Africa have been greatly underestimated, particularly when the compounding variables of state disintegration or enclave production are present, raising the question of its wisdom and sustainability. Somalia, Angola, Sierra Leone, and the Democratic Republic of the Congo all have proved much more recalcitrant than anticipated and have demanded levels of military commitment that few states are willing to contemplate.

When there has been civil war without state disintegration or another country's intervention, African leaders have favored international mediation, not intervention. This approach seems appropriate.

The difficult case would be when genocide occurs, for international conventions call for the African concern with sovereignty to be set aside in this case. Nonetheless, for reasons cited above, the conditions producing genocide are rare in Africa, and it probably is wrong to allow general policy for the continent to be driven by it. Much more likely to occur are incidents of ethnic cleansing (in which a group is expelled but extermination is not attempted). There are no clear conventions supporting interventions in these cases, and African states are certain to be highly resistant to any responses that violate the norms of sovereignty. For better or for worse, then, after-the-fact humanitarian interventions involving military force are not likely to be undertaken in such circumstances.

The most difficult class of cases involves state disintegration. Angola and Sierra Leone evoked attention because of the suffering of their own peoples. Also of concern, however, are situations in which one state's discord affects the security of its neighbor(s), as in the Congo-Rwanda rebellion, or in which one state is the base for rebel activity in a neighbor, as in the Congo-Uganda-Sudan triangle. States hosting rebel bases can be dealt with by mediation, but conflicts that arise out of state disintegration are a fundamental challenge to the existing international system, for they violate its basic premise of viable state actors. It is unclear how, if at all, the international system is going to respond to this challenge. The resource implications are great, and sadly, the refugees created by humanitarian crises in sub-Saharan Africa have little prospect of reaching the borders of rich countries.

The Prevention of Civil Conflict

Dealing with civil conflicts in Africa after they are already in progress is expensive and usually ineffective. Therefore they usually will be beyond the capacity of the UN or African regional organizations, and the major powers will be reluctant to become involved, prolonging these crises and making them still more expensive (in terms of both relief and military intervention).

The best approach, then, is to prevent the occurrence of these breakdowns. The work of the Collier group at the World Bank indicates that the chances of civil conflict increase by 40 percent if there has been a *resolved* conflict in the preceding period (and, of course, are substantially higher than that if peace was not restored).[6] An ounce of early prevention is worth two ounces of late prevention effort and at least a pound of cure for an existing conflict. As we indicated earlier, current research also indicates that social and economic grievances are not the driving causes of these disorders.[7] Although it certainly is desirable to address these grievances for their own sake, doing so is not an effective or efficient route for dealing with civil conflict. In any case, outside South Africa, inequality is not particularly severe in sub-Saharan Africa by international standards.

An effective method of prevention would be a system of international guarantees. We would propose treaty agreements between African governments and international groupings that guaranteed the regime against coup, invasion, or rebellion in return for minimal human rights, independent courts, and democracy. The commitment would *not* be to eradicate any rebellious pockets but to ensure that rebels would not take control of the government or of any enclave of significant export production.

Why would such a set of arrangements be desirable, and how might they be achieved? Sovereign states will make their own decisions about whether and how to enter into such agreements, and as a result, the final agreements they negotiate will look different from anything we propose. We would like to walk through the logic of our own thinking on the subject, however, in the hope that it may sharpen the thinking of diplomats as they reach for their own solutions. Our objective is to show how an idealist objective of helping Africa achieve its developmental potential might be achieved in a world in which the decisions of most states are driven by realist, self-interested considerations.[8]

At the moment, Africa is caught in a vicious circle. It cannot get the domestic and international investments it needs for development because the business community fears that its states are unstable and frequently predatory. But this instability and predation in turn are caused by underdevelopment—low GNP per capita and heavy dependence on the export of primary products, particularly from enclaves. The growth and diversification that would enable African countries to escape this structural underdevelopment cannot be achieved without investment. Something external, or exogenous, to this vicious logic is necessary to break out of the negative circle of causation.

The large-sample cross-national studies that have been done on the causes of civil disorder all support the foregoing analysis in that they agree that *structural* factors best predict vulnerability to civil conflict.

The three groups do differ with one another (and us) on precisely what those might be. We've already noted that Collier and the World Bank group emphasize dependence on the export of primary products. The State Failure Task Force suggests that on a *global* basis, low infant mortality rates and high involvement in international trade are associated with the lowest probability of civil conflict. Their *Africa* analysis also points to trade, but their other factors predicting conflict are a decline in GDP per capita and urbanization that is disproportionate to the level of economic development.[9] This list of factors suffers from being rather ad hoc and less justified by theory than suits our tastes. Fearon and Laitin give prominence to poverty and low growth, which they argue are proxy measures for weak states. They doubt the Collier group's emphasis on primary product export dependence. However, Fearon and Laitin do find evidence that oil producers may be more susceptible to civil conflict, which fits with our broader thesis that the factor driving civil conflict in Africa is dependence on enclave production (an interpretation to which they explicitly remain open).[10] For the purposes of the policy positions advocated in this book, however, what is important is not which of these structural variables is the driving factor behind vulnerability to civil conflict, but that *all of them* are beyond the near-term control of the political actors in a country and that the civil conflicts that result from them make it much less likely that performance on these variables can be improved. In short, all three analyses point to African states being caught in a vicious circle in which weak development leads to weak states and civil conflict, which in turn lead to poor economic growth. All three sets of studies, then, lend support to our argument that external support is appropriate to provide the assurance of stability that is key to renewed economic development for these states.

In Chapter 1, we argued that weak states contribute to the persistence of personal rule in Africa. We have just noted that Fearon and Laitin also see weak states as a root cause of civil conflict, and our quantitative analysis in the preceding chapter supports this point. It is thought that in the absence of effective states, ethnic groups are unable to make a convincing (or credible) commitment that they will compete with one another in the future according to nonviolent rules of the game, for there is no assurance the state will enforce the rules. In these circumstances, one group may be tempted to "take out" the other before it is strong enough to do the same to it. Thus the game theory literature on ethnic conflict generally assumes that an actual descent into violence is not in the interests of either party and occurs only because of this kind of "security dilemma" situation.[11]

It certainly is true that an interethnic riot or civil war is not in the interests of the greatest number of the members of either group. But John Mueller suggests that the actual perpetrators of the worst forms of attack on ethnic "others" generally are a minority, who may very well derive psychological or material benefits from their attacks, even while most of the members of the group they "represent" lose from them.[12] The case studies done on ethnic clashes also suggest that political opportunists and those who base their careers on building an ethnic identity (ethnic entrepreneurs) may gain from a conflict at the long-term expense of the group they lead.[13] Thus the breakdown of the state and the difficulty of making credible commitments for the enforcement of agreements is not only a problem for relations *between* groups but may well be a problem *within* them as well. The failure of states or the weakening of social institutions work at two levels to open the way to breakdown and violence. When states are weak, external guarantees of the rules of the game may provide the critical ingredient that enables groups to have confidence that they can continue to compete with each other peacefully.

Guarantees of stability for those countries that have not already broken down in conflict is the easiest and most efficient external factor to supply. As we demonstrated in Chapter 4, the driving cause of civil wars in Africa is not the social and economic grievances that often underlie them but the ease with which rebellion can be financed by capturing an export enclave, a port, or the international resources that come with holding the capital.[14] If the international system were able to guarantee that the legitimate government would not be overthrown by force of arms and that rebels would not be permitted to hold (and thus "tax") export enclaves, most of the motive force and finance for rebellion would disappear, and disaffected groups would not attempt it. There might be rural pockets of disorder, but they would be unable to grow, and the stability that businesses need before making investments would be assured.

A *credible commitment* of support by a group of powers with mobile, well-equipped strike forces and a good record of success in such ventures would be highly effective and efficient in guaranteeing stability. The experience of France with its former colonies between 1960 and 1990 suggests that very few groups in Africa (military or civilian) are willing to risk a rebellion when a regime is guaranteed by a European power.[15] (Britain's recent successful intervention in defense of Freetown in Sierra Leone carries a similar lesson.) Because the guarantees were credible, the cost to France of providing them were modest. However, France extended this protection in the service of its own narrow national interests and supported regimes that were undemocratic and sometimes unsavory. France has a reduced interest in providing the kinds of guarantees it did in the past.[16] A multilateral guarantee would be superior to a bilateral one in any case because it would be more likely to be based on broad humanitarian principles.

Prerequisites for Guarantees

Stability is not desirable in all circumstances for any kind of regime. We advocate guarantees only for democratic states that uphold a minimum level of human rights. Collier finds no evidence that democracy reduces the likelihood of a first occurrence of civil conflict.[17] Its relationship to economic development, particularly in low-income countries, also is unclear, but there seems to be no evidence that democracies actually hinder development.[18] However, the research of Ibrahim Elbadawi and Nicholas Sambanis suggests that democracy reduces the likelihood that civil conflict will *recur* after peace has been made.[19] Both the State Failure Task Force and Fearon and Laitin find that transitional democracies are more vulnerable to civil conflict than those that are either authoritarian or full democracies.[20] Thus by these two accounts, if African states are to be encouraged to make the transition from autocracy to democracy, they need guarantees for their stability as they move through the change and extra incentives to stay the course to full democracy, once they have begun on the path. One should add that democracy encourages greater attention to domestic grievances and provides an opportunity for legitimate political change. Without the prospect of change, disaffection is likely to continue to build, and there can be no humanitarian argument for keeping a regime in power.

Similar arguments apply to insisting on minimal human rights standards. The moral arguments for the protection of a regime and for insisting on nonviolent methods of change depend upon them. Furthermore, Fearon and Laitin find evidence that countries that engage in human rights abuses are more likely to find themselves subsequently in civil war.[21]

A final, related reason for insisting on these democratic and humanitarian standards is that the industrial democracies that would have to be involved in enforcement find that their own domestic political costs for intervention are much higher when the beneficiary nation is not morally attractive—and the credibility of the commitment to ensure stability is thereby reduced.[22]

But what is democracy? For most of the U.S. policy community, the answer is multiparty competition and internationally monitored free elections. Other parts of the world have been less sure. At one extreme, there are presidents who meet these formal criteria but still have manipulated the system and either lack or subsequently have lost the confidence of their electorates. It would not be desirable to have international guarantees used to maintain such unpopular presidents in office against a popular challenge. At the other end of the spectrum, widely popular presidents do come to office by other democratic routes than these formal criteria. National conventions drawn from all organized sectors of the society (but without elections) were important to democratic change in Francophone Africa in the late 1980s, and massive demonstrations such as the People's Power movement in the Philippines were critical at other junctures. Even though these alternative mechanisms are more vulnerable to manipulation than multiparty elections (as President Mobutu of the Democratic Republic of Congo, then Zaire, skillfully showed in the early 1990s), they also can carry deep legitimacy. The important points to emphasize are that (1) presidents who have lost the support of their electorates not be able to use international guarantees to extend their terms in office, (2) change of governments be accomplished without the use of force, (3) the regimes that are the beneficiaries of international guarantees be well known, and (4) those guarantees be available quickly and reliably when a regime is challenged by force of arms. Since we advocate that each country negotiate for its own set of guarantees, it is possible for the details of these agreements to vary and for the standards for human rights and democracy to change over time—we hope for the better.

The possibility of guarantees, moreover, would help to attract many regimes toward adopting more democratic practices and respecting minimal human rights. Many presidents in sub-Saharan Africa are more worried about coups, invasions, and rebellions than they are about electoral opposition and would regard multiparty and electoral guarantees as an attractive trade-off. Similarly, ethnic cleansing most often is a strategy for retaining power. Presidents who would lose international protection when the "tribal card" was abused would be less likely to use it.

Note that the international sanction for authoritarianism and ethnic cleansing would not be intervention but the withdrawal of protection. Regimes that abused these norms would more easily fall victim to domestic forces that would replace them. Democratic and humanitarian regimes, in contrast, would be sustained. Thus there would be a gradual "ratcheting up" of democracy and respect for human rights.

We think that an independent judiciary needs to be part of the conditions for a guarantee as well. Prospective investors fear predation, not only from rebels but from governments as well. Fixed and dedicated capital investments are particularly vulnerable because of their asset specificity, and this fact has restricted the kinds of businesses that various firms are interested in pursuing in Africa. Substantial investment and diversification cannot be achieved under these conditions. Independent judiciaries are necessary to guarantee the inviolability of contracts and to ensure that dedicated assets will not be subject to ex post predation. It is in the developmental interests of African states to bind themselves to autonomous courts.

Because these guarantees of regime stability would be extended through treaty between *individual* African countries and an international grouping, they would respect the norm of sovereignty. This aspect is crucial to their acceptance by African states and the non-NATO members of the United Nations. No country would or could be forced to sign such an agreement. And if an African government chose to terminate an agreement or to violate its terms for democracy, human rights, or the judiciary, the sanction would be the public loss of the guarantees of its stability. The international system would not invade; the local government would simply immediately become more vulnerable to coup or rebellion. These guarantees are not, then, a variant of neocolonialism, where external powers assume suzerainty. Instead, by increasing the prospects for democracy, human rights, and autonomous courts, such an agreement *increases* the responsiveness of African governments to their own peoples and their stability in pursuing this sovereign path.

Guarantors

We suggested earlier that a multilateral guarantee would be superior to a bilateral one. The interests served are less likely to be narrowly selfish. Furthermore, the credibility of the commitment would be increased if there were multiple guarantors, any one of which has the capability and motivation to act if stability were threatened. Nonetheless, a commitment by the UN or the African Union would not enforce democracy and would not offer a credible deterrent because they have past records of ineffective intervention, they require the negotiation of broad coalitions before acting, and a majority of their members are not democracies. The efforts of the Clinton administration to get African states to create a rapid-deployment strike force were flawed for the same reasons.

Similarly the United States (and thus NATO) would not be a suitable power for such guarantees, as it has been notably reluctant to accept losses where its national interests are not at stake. Its commitment therefore would not be credible, and as a consequence it would be more likely to be tested—as it was in Somalia—with greater loss of human life. Nigeria, in concert with ECOWAS, made commendable if flawed attempts to bring order to Liberia and Sierra Leone, but the very fact that it failed makes any guarantees that it alone would extend less credible and therefore less effective in preventing civil conflict. The certainty that a guarantee would be honored if it were challenged and that sufficient force would be provided to nip the coup or rebellion quickly is crucial to the guarantee's effectiveness, to its being rarely used, and to a minimal cost and loss of life when it is.

A group of African democracies and European powers would be the best candidates for providing these guarantees. Fortunately, the two regional hegemons in Africa—South Africa and Nigeria—are now democratic, have shown a willingness to play this kind of role in the past, and could provide their military muscle to support a group of states that included, for example, Botswana, Ghana, Mali, and Senegal.

The effectiveness of such a group would be greatly enhanced, however, if it were supported by European powers. (Canada is a possibility as well because it has been a leader in multinational peacekeeping in recent years.) The Western European Union (WEU; essentially NATO without the United States) is trying to create a rapid-deployment strike force at the moment, and its participation would add considerable credibility. The European states involved have been looking for a mission that would justify the need for an independent military force and overcome U.S. unease at its loss of control. One would need to ensure, however, that such a large alliance was able to act quickly and reliably when the security of an African government was threatened. Bilateral guarantees could be less unwieldy.

The Nordic states are accepted in Africa as having acted consistently in the interests of the continent rather than their national self-interests and therefore would be even more acceptable to Africans than the WEU. However, the Swedes have positioned themselves as mediators, not enforcers in the international system, making it unlikely that they would agree to play such a guarantor role.[23] Norway has been willing to play a wider role in peacekeeping, and it and Denmark might be better candidates.

Alternatively, France and Britain might take on this responsibility for their respective spheres of historical influence in Africa. The fact that they are former colonial powers would offend the political sensibilities of many Africans, but better alternatives may be hard to come by. Most Francophone African states have accepted guarantees from France in the past.[24] Properly speaking, what is being guaranteed and how should be a bigger issue than who provides it. Since the guarantees would be provided through treaty arrangements with each African state, it is not strictly necessary that the same group of powers be involved in every treaty. It may well be that a different pattern of arrangements would be necessary for Anglophone states and former French colonies, for example.

We do not want to suggest that these former colonial powers have always been altruistic in their past African interventions. For example, France has been accused of fostering an uprising that suited its own interests on at least one occasion, and its commercial interests probably have been advanced by the larger number of interventions it has undertaken.[25] French oil interests in Cameroon, Congo-Brazzaville, and Gabon are such that they are likely to override any conflicting commitment to democracy. The proposals we are making here may not change that fact, but they also are unlikely to exacerbate it. However, France's interests in Senegal and Mali seem quite compatible with the maintenance of democracy in those states. Involvement by France in public multilateral guarantees of these particular democracies clearly would be different in both character and effect. Where the interests of a former colonial power are well aligned with the protection of democratic regimes, it should be seen as an opportunity, not a problem.

Nonetheless, it does follow that a central role for African states in the guarantee function is important to its legitimacy and to ensure the appropriateness of the purposes it will be likely to serve. A collectivity of states should be involved as guarantors. Alliances can be unwieldy and slow if they require consensus and coordination before action is taken—and such attributes would seriously inhibit the credibility of the commitment that was being made and is needed for stability. Thus any treaties developed probably would need to leave open the possibility of uncoordinated action. For example, treaties might provide that if a guaranteed government requests assistance in dealing with a coup or rebellion and a majority of the guarantors agree within twenty-four hours that it is a legitimate request, *any* of the guaranteeing states would be free to respond.

Whatever the grouping of states, the important points are that (1) it would respond *reliably* and *quickly* to any threat to a guaranteed democratic regime, (2) its combined military forces would be well-equipped and highly mobile, and (3) it has a deserved reputation for completing what it has begun. All these points are essential to credibility, which is what creates effectiveness and keeps costs and loss of life minimal. It is perfectly acceptable for the group of guaranteeing states to deliberate for an extended period on whether to sign a treaty of guarantee, but once a treaty is in place and a challenge occurs, the response must be immediate and without the possibility of veto or procrastination because of self-interested reservations by one of the guarantors.

Credible Commitments

There is a considerable literature on credible commitments, but it is an imperfect fit for the problem we are addressing here. Most of the thinking on the subject in political science and international relations concerns nuclear deterrence, but some of the insights about alliances are useful.[26] The economics literature on credible commitment is largely concerned with the enforcement of commercial contracts, but the New Institutional Economists have explored the problem of binding governments to their economic policy promises.[27] These lesser literatures provide some useful analytic tools.

A standard mechanism for enhancing the credibility of a commitment is the placement of "trip wires"—stationing troops in the country to which the guarantee is being extended.[28] The classic pattern in Africa has been for a European power to have a rotating but continuous small number of troops on training exercises in a country whose stability it wishes to ensure. The facts that these forces would be at risk in any disturbance, that they could respond to it quickly, and that major powers rarely abandon their personnel when they are attacked all combine to heighten credibility.

The problem of credibility interacts in a potentially perverse way with the desirability of having international guarantors who are committed to *Africa's* best interests. Why should any state agree to commit its resources and the lives of its soldiers if its national interests are not advanced thereby? And how credible would such a commitment be if they were not? (Wouldn't the architects of potential coups and rebellions reason that disinterested guarantors could be easily frightened off with a surgical show of brutal force, as the United States was in Somalia, thereby undermining the crucial credibility of the commitment?) This conundrum is less severe for the African guarantors, for they gain directly from containing disorder in their region.

Why should any European nation wish to pay the costs of guarantee, however? The credibility and effectiveness of our idealist objective requires an answer that can stand up to realist objections. We should observe first that these costs would not be very large—the more credible the commitment, the less often it would be tested, and the first line of response in any case might come from the African members of the alliance. Low costs have typically been a condition of Western intervention.[29] But costs are still costs, and the credibility that they will be paid when needed increases with the degree to which vital national interests of the guarantor are involved. Although French costs in providing stability to its former African colonies were modest, they were not trivial. France has maintained a *force d'action rapide* (FAR) ready at home and has intervened thirty times since the 1960s. It has suppressed riots and coups and committed forces against rebel groups.[30]

The presence of substantial business investments in an African country increases the willingness of a European power to intervene to protect them. This need not be bad, as Africa is much in need of foreign private investment. France served as a guarantor of African regimes for precisely this reason and was more credible for doing so. But whatever the benefits in economic growth and civil order that came from French intervention, it did little to promote democracy, good government, or human rights, and its motives were sometimes quite crass.[31] One option would be to have France, Britain, or the Western European Union sell insurance to their own companies to guard against private investment losses caused by civil conflict in selected *democratic* African countries. The insurance would be available only for African states that meet minimal standards of democracy, human rights, and judicial autonomy and are willing to sign treaties to protect them. The insurance would be nullified (or the insured amount dramatically reduced) if the country itself failed to keep to these standards and the treaty were canceled. The businesses themselves then would have an interest in the maintenance of democracy and human rights in the country, and the European power would have an interest in intervening to protect both its businesses and the insurance it was providing.

Such insurance would create a "stock of value" that a guarantor state would lose if it failed to keep its commitments, which makes the assurances more credible, of course. But why should the political leaders in an African state whose stability has been guaranteed keep *their* commitments to democracy, human rights, and an independent judiciary, particularly if public opinion turns against them or foreign investments have created a substantial prize on which they could prey?

The answer is that it is easier to secure investments than democracy. If the judicial process is abrogated and contracts are not honored, the regime would lose its guarantees and become vulnerable to coups and rebellions. Predation alone is unlikely to be sufficient to cause governments to renege on their promises. But if the leaders think they are going to lose the next election, then loss of protection if democracy is abrogated is not much of a threat—after all, a near certainty is more threatening than a possibility. Or is it?

There is good reason to believe that the package of foreign guarantees, democracy, human rights, judicial independence, and insured business investments will prove mutually reinforcing. The usual African president who is tempted to rig the next election has an elite with few expectations of democracy and little experience in how to succeed at it, a carefully monitored and handpicked officer corps in the army, a harassed opposition, a weak press, a subservient judiciary, and a business community that tailored its investments to predatory autocracy. Thus the moves this president makes to abrogate democracy will meet with little opposition.

A president who has made a treaty commitment to democracy, human rights, and an autonomous judiciary in return for international guarantees of the regime, however, faces a very different political terrain when attempting to renege. The very attempt of the president to abandon democracy will signal personal doubts about his or her popularity, which will affect the calculations of all the other actors. Other members of the elite will have factored democracy into their political plans, and even some members of the cabinet may defect. Because the army was asked to protect a democracy, it will be hard to gauge the loyalties of the officers to an unpopular autocrat. An opposition will be organized, easily mobilized, and have access to a press that will be hard to control. Some resistance can be expected from the courts, and diplomatic pressures will be mobilized. Finally, the economy will have grown under democratic guarantees and the insurance we propose. Thus an authoritarian direction will hurt tax revenues, and business-people can be expected to resist a change that would lessen the value of their insurance. In short, multiple forces will push the regime back toward democracy, once it has made the kind of commitment we advo-cate. Something very similar happened in Zambia, when President Frederick Chiluba tried to amend the constitution to give himself a third term. He was thwarted, and others can be as well.

To use Kenneth Shepsle's terms, the initial commitment of African presidents to democracy under our proposals is "motivational"—they do it because they believe in democracy and want to ensure their own continued governance under that system. But once the commitment has been institutionalized, it becomes "imperative"—because forces come into existence that enforce it.[32] In other respects, the process here is similar to, if less powerful than, that which occurred in England fol-lowing its Civil War. Parliament gained the power to audit and veto the Crown's expenditures and to force it to pay its debts. As Nahalel Nel-lis puts it, "The Crown's agreement with Parliament became self-enforcing because the changes resulted in greater commerce *and* gen-erated revenue for the Crown. The English Crown thus had no incentive to violate this legal regime."[33]

None of these countervailing forces will stop a *popular* president with an authoritarian bent and a public ready to abandon democracy in the pursuit of other goals. This scenario should actually reassure those who worry that international guarantees could compromise sover-eignty. The mechanisms we are proposing reinforce the responsiveness of a regime to its people and provide a path away from the current undemocratic alliances between enclaves and autocrats.

The exact coalition of guarantors can be quite variable, as can the mechanisms whereby their commitments are made credible. Obviously, some arrangements have much more attractive features for Africa than others do. The major benefits come from credible guarantees against civil conflict for democratic and humane African states, not so much from the details. The international and regional powers in a position to provide such assurances will of course negotiate what they are willing to do according to their own normative and material interests.

A set of credible multilateral guarantees for democratic regimes would provide an appropriate set of incentives to advance better gov-ernment in many African states. If it had been in place to provide guar-antees to the newly elected Hutu government in Burundi in the early

1990s, it would have prevented the takeover by the Tutsi military (and possibly the assassination of the president that preceded it), the outbreak of the current civil war there, and the cascading human rights abuses that followed. In doing so, it might very well have averted the genocide that overtook Rwanda as well, for the Hutu leaders there drew from Burundi the lesson that the Tutsi would not respect democracy. It is hard to see an exit from the current impasses in Burundi and Rwanda without credible international guarantees for both democracy and the protection of minority rights. But such after-the-fact guarantees are less effective and much more costly than firm preventive ones would have been.

Genocide is the only circumstance in which existing international treaties *oblige* states to override norms of sovereignty and intervene. But the United Nations and the international system failed to meet that obligation in Rwanda, with cataclysmic results. By creating a rapid-response force trained for use in Africa and stationed on the continent, bilateral guarantees against coups and rebellions would also make it *possible*—and thus more likely—for an international grouping to respond quickly to any threats of genocide in any country in the region.

Conclusion

Africa is likely to be a site for major international humanitarian interventions in the coming years, as it has been already—but not for the reasons usually assumed. Ethnic tensions are a part of the background, not the cause of humanitarian disasters in Africa. And the cases of ethnic persecution that do occur are unlikely to be amenable to international intervention because of the strong commitment of African states to the principle of the inviolability of sovereignty. The larger number of African calls for humanitarian intervention instead are likely to come in response to state collapse, prompted by weak states and enclave, extractive forms of wealth generation. These types of intervention have proved to be much more demanding militarily than the international system's image of African weakness had led it to expect. Thus the willingness of the international system to commit the resources that are needed to deal with state collapses that have already occurred is doubtful. Since follow-through is unlikely and the path to effectiveness is unclear, it may well be best for the international system to avoid intervention altogether in the face of state collapse—for doing so may only perpetuate the conflict and increase the loss of human life.

Therefore the international community must commit to *preventing* state collapse, coups, and rebellions from happening in the first place. Bilateral treaties between individual African democracies and a grouping of African and European democracies that obligated the latter to intervene against challenges to the former regimes would be highly effective at providing substantially enhanced civil order in Africa and creating incentives toward more democracy. In doing so, they would also create environments in which foreign investment would be more secure and economic development more likely.

The system of guarantees we have suggested would not deal with the humanitarian crises and civil conflicts of all countries on the continent. It is important to recognize that not all problems are amenable to solution at the present time, that the "perfect" can be the enemy of the "substantially better," and that unrealistically ambitious commitments can be a source of miscalculation and war.

This regime of guarantees does recognize the central role that the international system already has in maintaining state sovereignty in Africa. The frequent incidence on the continent of juridical statehood in the absence of its empirical prerequisites is a manifestation of international power without responsibility. Guarantees render the international system responsible and visible in the exercise of its power. But they also create a framework of incentives for African political leaders that make them more responsive to their own populations and are conducive to peace, democracy, and economic growth. In these senses, guarantees would work to enhance the ability of Africans themselves to influence their own destinies.

6

Conclusion

I N TITLING THIS BOOK *AFRICA'S STALLED DEVELOPMENT,* WE REFLECTED THE deep disappointment on the continent and abroad with four decades of postindependence rule. By labeling Africa's development as "stalled," we do not mean to imply that the continent is a "basket case," as is often said, or to suggest that every country on the continent has suffered the same fate. Botswana's success and that of a half-dozen other countries are testaments to real progress. But on balance, Africa's development has fallen far short of what it might have been. With the exceptions duly noted, the continent's economies have been slow to grow at best, and more often are stuck in decades-long depressions. Although it is better today than under colonialism, the general welfare of Africans has not come close to meeting expectations. And today the continent is home to the world's greatest concentration of civil conflicts, some of which have persisted for years. Overall, the postindependence development record is a disappointment, and deep structural changes to reverse it are in order.

It is equally important, however, to resist a cultural explanation of these problems, one that would blame Africa's problems on social pathologies endemic to the continent. A theme that we have stressed throughout this book is that there are historical and structural reasons why Africa's development project has stalled over the last forty years. Moreover, we have emphasized that Africa's connections with the international system are central to the negative dynamics described in these pages. This argument is not a reformulation of dependency theory, which reigned in the 1970s. That approach held that the international system benefited at the expense of peripheral regions and tended to assign little agency to local actors themselves. Our emphasis is not on powerful leaders in the developed world who exploit the poor. Although exploitation exists, we doubt the developed world derives much benefit from Africa's present condition—and it would gain much more from vibrant African economies and strong states. Our argument is instead that Africa's interactions with the international system perpetuate the negative dynamics that are at the heart of the continent's problems—even when, as with foreign aid and technical assistance, world actors are trying to be of help.

In contemporary African studies, the central paradigm for understanding politics on the continent is what we have termed the "personal rule system." We have not substantially diverged from the picture of political life that this paradigm provides. However, in our analysis, the focus was on where the politics of personal rule come from and how they are sustained over time. To that end, we argued that personal rule does not primarily grow out of a particular African culture, nor is it a response to Africa's ethnic heterogeneity, though these factors may matter in some instances. Rather, the features commonly associated with personal rule are maintained by the weakness of African states, which itself is a legacy of colonial institutions; by an international system that rewards statehood in name but not in practice, which also contributes to the weakness of African states; and by a particularly narrow economic structure that depends on the export of goods generated in enclaves, in particular natural resources.

As we demonstrated in Chapters 1 and 4, many African economies are dependent on enclave production—both in its traditional form of mineral extraction and estate agriculture and the "softer" form of foreign aid and remittances from diasporic labor. The political significance of enclave production is that it allows elites to collect rents—taxes, bribes, and even consultancies—without having to contribute to the general productivity of society. These rents are easily turned into patronage, and they militate against developing capable states, broad-based legitimacy, or national communities. In that way, enclave production reinforces the limited institutions produced by colonialism as well as a personal rule form of politics. Indeed, we contended that the export of high-value items is an important foundation for the various negative features associated with personal rule. International actors may not desire this outcome, but Africa's interactions with the international system have created a set of incentives for African leaders that are deeply dysfunctional to the continent's development. Africa will remain mired in underdevelopment until these incentives can be fundamentally restructured.

In Chapter 2, we argued that the combination of debt and overseas development assistance exacerbates this structural vulnerability of African systems. Most African countries are saddled with international debts that they have no prospect of repaying and are able to keep current only through high levels of ODA. The combination provides no incentive to African leaders to avoid unwise policies and causes them to orient their attentions externally to the international system rather than internally to the productivity and welfare of their own populations. In fact, the current extreme dependence on ODA is quite dysfunctional to governance in Africa. The thrust of reform should be to restructure the conditions under which African leaders work, so that there are incentives for better outcomes.

Thus we support Jubilee 2000 in advocating that most of Africa's international debts be written off. We see this as a high developmental priority for the continent, and one in which the international system can make a crucial difference. At a minimum, debt must be reduced to a level at which no ODA needs to be recycled to pay it. Debt cancellation also should be accompanied by a comparable reduction (but not elimination) in total levels of ODA. Foreign aid must not dominate the income strategies of elites and must be modest and concentrated on infrastructure and human welfare. In the long run, the elimination of debt and reduction of aid will change the incentives for African elites and stimulate their efforts to develop broad-based economies that can generate their own internal revenue. We believe that this change, as well as a move away from enclave dependency, will likely make the negative dynamics of personal rule costly for African leaders over the long run, and they will move away from it.

Technical assistance (TA) has had a similarly corrosive structural effect on Africa. The norms of development assistance in the fifty years after World War II created a two-track personnel system in poor countries, with international technical assistants paid U.S. salaries and domestic employees paid local ones that could be less than one-tenth as much. This norm prevailed even when the two sets of personnel were doing the same work and when locals had a superior capacity to make development initiatives sustainable. Local professionals therefore had a strong incentive to work outside their home countries (where they would be paid U.S. wages) or to supplement their salaries by corruption.

In the 1990s, this two-track norm weakened somewhat, so that locals are increasingly hired by foreign development organizations at wages that approach international standards. This change does not wholly address the problem, however. It still encourages local professionals to work for international agencies (including NGOs) rather than domestic ones, and it leaves them responsible to international rather than local agendas. A set of proposals are advanced in Chapter 3 and the two appendixes, whereby ODA can be used to create cadres of exceptional local professionals who work for domestic organizations and are responsible to their own people but receive international wages, as long as they conduct themselves with integrity and high professional standards.

Neither the ODA nor TA proposals made here wholly eliminate the problems of structural dependence, which are so central to Africa's dysfunctional development path, but they do relieve them and significantly increase local responsibility. In this way, they turn ODA and TA from being an aspect of the problem to being part of the solution.

In focusing on the civil conflicts that are so prominent in Africa now, we argued that weak states and enclave export production contribute to the feasibility of waging war. Contrary to the dominant way of approaching conflict in Africa, we contended that ethnicity itself is not the cause of conflict: Africans do not fight because of perceived cultural differences between themselves or because of innate hatred. Ethnicity can be mobilized during conflict in Africa and can shape its contours, but ethnicity is rarely its source. Rather, in Chapter 4 we endorse the insight of Paul Collier and his associates that focuses on the economic and other structural foundations that allow civil conflict to be prosecuted. But in refining the Collier thesis, we found enclave production, not the export of primary products, to be the key structural foundation for civil conflict—in particular, sustained civil conflict. Enclave dependency is crucial because enclaves produce enough revenue to finance wars and reward elites even in the midst of the widespread devastation caused by civil conflict. Not every civil conflict in Africa is sustained through an enclave economic structure. In particular, the Great Lakes conflicts in Rwanda and Burundi seem not to depend on enclave production. But we argue that a significant proportion of African civil conflicts persist because of the structural particularities of their economies.

Africa is unlikely to be any more or less prone to Rwandan-style mass violence than the rest of the world. However, our analysis of civil conflict suggests that sustained civil conflicts financed through (mostly mineral) enclave production—as in Angola, Sierra Leone, the Democratic Republic of Congo, Liberia, and other countries—are likely to remain a feature of the African landscape. This prediction prompts a proposal that would allow some members of the international system to help Africa escape the vicious circle in which a significant number of its states are currently caught (see Chapter 5).

The starting point for this analysis is the recognition that dealing with these crises after they are already in progress is expensive and ineffective. Thus, trying to end these conflicts will be beyond the capacity of the UN or African regional organizations, and the major powers will be reluctant to become involved, prolonging these crises and making them still more expensive (in terms of both relief and military intervention).

The priority, then, is to prevent the occurrence of these breakdowns in the first place. Current research indicates that social and economic grievances are not the driving causes of these conflicts. Although it certainly is desirable to address these grievances for their own sake, doing so is not an effective or efficient route for dealing with civil conflict.

The states most vulnerable to breakdown are those that rely on enclave production, particularly of natural resources. The income produced in these enclaves is easily attached, either by the government or by rebels, even when the productive capacity of the population at large is being destroyed by civil war. Thus dissidents have an incentive to rebel, and governments have no incentive to invest in the economic and social infrastructure that would produce prosperity for the general population. This feature of the political economy of many African states is structural and unlikely to change in the intermediate future.

In these circumstances, treaty agreements between individual African governments and an international grouping of African and European states that guaranteed the regime against coup or rebellion in return for minimal human rights, democracy, and an independent judiciary could be highly attractive. A credible commitment of support by such a group of powers would be highly effective and efficient. The experience of France with its former colonies between 1960 and 1990 suggests that very few groups (military or civilian) are willing to risk a rebellion when a regime is guaranteed by a European power. Thus it cost the French relatively little to give guarantees to its newly independent colonies. France had a different agenda than the one motivating this book in providing these guarantees and in any case no longer has as strong an interest in providing them. A multilateral guarantee would be superior to a bilateral one, because it would be more likely to be based on broad humanitarian principles. Nonetheless, a commitment by the UN or the African Union would not enforce democracy and would not offer a credible deterrent because they have a past record of ineffective intervention. Hence the argument for a more ad hoc group of African and European democracies.

Guarantees for nondemocratic regimes are undesirable because they do not encourage attention to domestic grievances or provide an opportunity for legitimate political change. The possibility of guarantees, however, would help to induce many regimes to adopt more democratic practices. Many presidents are more worried about coups and rebellions than they are about electoral opposition and would regard multiparty and electoral guarantees as an attractive trade-off. The credibility of the commitment by the European partners to these agreements would be enhanced if they insured the private investments of their nationals in the countries that had a treaty with them guaranteeing democracy.

Because these guarantees would be extended through treaty between *individual* African countries and an international grouping, they would respect the norm of sovereignty. African states would enter and exit these agreements voluntarily. Their effect would be to improve the responsiveness of African governments to their own peoples and to improve economic development.

Such arrangements would provide an appropriate set of incentives to advance good governance in many African states. By creating a European and African rapid-response force trained for use in Africa, such guarantees would also make it *possible* for an international grouping to respond quickly to any threats of genocide—which is the only circumstance in which existing international treaties *oblige* states to override norms of sovereignty and intervene.

An underlying contention running through the book is that a narrow economic base (enclaves oriented toward foreign export) has proven disastrous for sub-Saharan Africa. This economic base has dovetailed with high dependence on foreign aid, crippling foreign debts, and a colonial legacy of domestic weak states in order to support a host of negative dynamics in Africa. We have focused particularly on personal rule and susceptibility to conflict and put forward some concrete proposals for how the developed world might change its relationship to Africa for the better.

The analytical approach pursued here has stressed the way in which particular structural environments create incentives and opportunities for action. Thus, lucrative, easily cashed goods from enclaves offer opportunities for corruption that do not jeopardize the source of revenues over time. The counterpoint is that broad-based national economies will over the long run create a different set of incentives—ones that will increase the costs of personal rule and decrease the risks of conflict.

Though not the subject of this book, a more favorable economic agenda would aim toward diversified small and medium farm and industrial production. Development on the continent is unlikely to produce deep or lasting benefits without this kind of economic basis. The economies of Ghana and Senegal created the kind of dynamics in which significant economic reform could be sustained and produce the political transformations that have led to democratic changes in government. But even these democracies are caught in a dysfunctional debt-aid trap and need international guarantees. Movement of Africa's severely enclave-dependent economies toward this kind of "rent-resistant" diversification will require incentives and foreign direct private investment—which also will require breaking out of the debt-aid syndrome and providing guarantees for the democracies that emerge. The incentives governing the systems must be transformed by a new set of relationships with the international system. We have made several proposals here, but more remain to be made.

When faced with such a wide range of problems—civil conflict, corruption, debt, AIDS, and so on—there is a temptation to throw up one's hands in desperation. But it is worth remembering that if Africa in general today presents a bleak picture, the crisis in which the continent finds itself is not entirely of its own making. The international system has worked to throw a blanket of negative incentives over the continent's elites—sometimes out of the malign motives of the world's powers, sometimes out of munificence, but most often simply out of ignorance and indifference. If African leaders are to be able and motivated to respond to the needs of their own peoples and militate against the current context of stalled development, the industrialized world must do its part to change the environment in which those leaders now operate. Once the incentives are set right, Africa has an ample supply of intelligent, talented, and dedicated men and women who will respond.

APPENDIX A

A Proposal to Set Salaries for African Civil Servants in Response to Competitive External Offers

THE FOLLOWING PROPOSAL IS ONE WAY IN WHICH TO MEET THE FOUR objectives set out in Chapter 3. Another is contained in Appendix B. One should consider these proposals in the first instance simply as illustrations. They illuminate the analysis offered and indicate some of the kinds of things that might be attempted in response. If the underlying argument is found plausible, the next steps would be to refine it further through research and international consultation, followed by its experimental implementation in selected countries and sectors.

1. African public service commissions should begin to set salaries in a manner similar to that of competitive institutions of higher education in the United States; that is, they should begin to meet bona fide competitive offers for personnel who provide critical services. (These regulations should apply to expatriates and locals alike, so as to create equity and alleviate the expatriate-local jealousy.)

Thus, if a local civil servant received a genuine offer from abroad or from a local institution outside government and if that official were judged by the country's public service commission to be supplying services that were important to the public welfare and were of a caliber unlikely to be provided by the likely successor in the position, that salary would be matched, with adjustments for the permanence and location of the position. A temporary position would have a certain percentage premium over a permanent one, and a person would be paid a lower salary to work in his or her home country than abroad. (Essentially, these are the same principles that some of the best technical assistance agencies apply in setting salaries for the expatriates they hire to send abroad. For example, one takes the in-country base salary and adds 10 percent plus certain expenses to send the person abroad. Conversely, one would *deduct* a similar percentage from foreign job offers in determining a local salary. If, say, an American and a Kenyan both had U.S. job offers at $50,000, such an agency would pay the American $55,000 to work in Kenya and the Kenyan $45,000.)

2. An added feature would be that positions above a certain level would be open to lateral recruitment from outside the civil service, with the salary paid being that which was being earned outside, plus a recruitment or promotion bonus.

3. Correspondingly, international donors should open their technical assistance positions to locals as well as expatriates, with salary scales that are designed to match demand for given levels of skill and performance to supply and with a foreign posting allowance the sole difference between local and expatriate salaries.

There are a number of advantages to this set of proposals, beyond that of breaking down the artificial and possibly racist boundary between expatriate and local wages. First, it would be possible to keep talented civil servants at home and in the public sector.

Second, the mechanism for adjusting salaries would be depoliticized, for it would work on a case-by-case basis in response to competitive pressures. No general arguments about equity or justice would be made, only about market forces. There would be no kickbacks to pay, for the local salary would be only that which one had demonstrated one could get elsewhere. (As the recipient would be receiving no economic rents, there would be none to share.)

Third, civil servants who wanted to advance would now see that the way to do so would be to demonstrate skills that would make them attractive to those outside the public sector looking for managerial talent. In effect, then, the truly talented and ambitious public officials would now try to impress donors, NGOs, and private corporations as well as their governments if they wanted to get ahead. To do so, they would have to demonstrate attributes of skill, diligence, honesty, wisdom, and effectiveness that frequently have not been adequately rewarded in the public sector. Note that these incentive effects would apply not only to those who actually received such competitive salary bonuses but even more so to those who were aspiring to them. These incentive payments would have a substantial multiplier effect.

4. A provision could be adopted that when, say, 75 percent of those in a certain job classification were receiving more than the standard civil service salary for those in that classification, the salaries of everyone in the classification would rise to the level of the lowest "outside offer" salary.

The advantage of this provision is that it would give civil servants who have not been busy hustling external offers a reason not to resist the efforts of those who have.

5. Initially, the extra salary costs of meeting competitive offers could be financed by a donor pool. Donors would benefit from having a better group of local development managers available to work on their projects and would have lower costs than if they had hired expatriate personnel.

It is likely that in the long run, such a scheme would pay for itself. Pressures for generalized increases in civil service salaries would be reduced and thus the rate of inflation in the public sector wages would be diminished (or more accurately, the rate of deflation would accelerate somewhat). Those civil servants who occupied posts for which there was no external demand would find their real wages declining and would leave the public sector. Potential new recruits would not find these posts attractive any longer, and thus the rate of inflation in public sector employment and wages would be slowed.

APPENDIX B

An "International Grand Corps" of African Public Service Professionals

W E ADVANCE A RADICAL PROPOSAL FOR GIVING STRENGTH AND AUTONomy to the professions in the public service in Africa.[1] It would need to be refined and advanced by Africans themselves if international organizations were to take it seriously. Thus we put it forward, not as a finished proposal but as the germ of an idea for African professionals to develop if they feel it has merit.

At the moment professionalism in African civil services is undermined by two major factors:

1. Africa is being drained of its best talent by the siren call of international salaries for those who are widely recognized as exceptional. Public servants who could do far greater good at home than they are likely to achieve working overseas, even in international development organizations, are leaving the continent.

2. Those professionals who do remain in their home countries generally suffer from a lack of autonomy, a factor so important to the generation of professionalism that it is generally used as part of its definition. In most African states, for most of the professions, there are few viable alternatives outside the public sector for those who fall from political grace. This factor makes professional public servants timid and conservative in their behavior. They become so anxious to avoid offending their political masters that they actually do not serve them very well.

Our proposal for dealing with these problems is inspired by the prestigious corporate bodies of professionals in the French civil service known as the "grand corps." Each of these corps recruits its members through an exceedingly competitive selection process that brings in the best candidates. Although each of these corps is responsible for certain distinct state tasks, they are not necessarily their most important functions. Instead, they compete with one another to provide government ministers with staff who can enjoy their confidence. These appointees serve at the full discretion of the political leadership and provide them with most of their policy advice and administrative assistance. No matter where they serve, however, members of the grand corps derive their salaries from their corps and not their positions.

Individuals in a grand corps who enjoy the confidence of the political leadership will serve in the most important policymaking positions in the government; those whose views are out of favor at the moment will hold more routine posts in the civil service and constitute a kind of administrative and policy "staff in waiting," who will be available when the political winds change.

Both those who enjoy the political confidence of the moment and those who do not have tenure in their corps and receive similar salaries. This material security encourages members of the grand corps to maintain high professional standards, be innovative, and take risks, which serves well both society and the government of the day. However, the fact that these elite administrators only hold positions that are critical to public policy when they have the confidence of the political leadership ensures political responsiveness.[2]

African governments would be well served if they were to have available to them a similar group of highly talented and professional higher civil servants who were politically responsive and adaptive to policy change. Something similar to this proposal was implemented by the United Nations in the Caribbean.[3]

Specifically, then, we propose that for each profession an Africa-wide grand corps be created with the following attributes:

1. Members of the corps itself would nominate people for candidate membership who had the appropriate minimum qualifications for their profession, who had five to ten years of public sector work experience, and who were judged to have been outstanding in their performance of those duties—both as to technical quality and as to the "publicness" of values served.

2. Those elected by the senior members of the corps to become candidate members would attend a professional upgrading course of, say, two months duration with all of the other candidates of that year. The course would contribute to professional competence but would also build peer ties. Upon successful completion of the course, which would not be guaranteed but which would be usual, the candidate would become a junior member of the corps.

3. Junior members would receive a substantial supplement to their incomes as long as they were in the service of an African government or (possibly) an indigenous nongovernmental organization. They also would be guaranteed a post in an international organization (UN, International Bank for Reconstruction and Development, World Health Organization, etc.) if their careers became blocked despite their having performed their duties at a high level of professional competence. The former provision would encourage them to continue working in poorly paid positions without turning to corruption or private business for supplemental sources of income. The latter provision would encourage both risk taking and adherence to professional standards and ethics, for being faithful to them would give them security. Thus these provisions would promote professional autonomy within the structure of the civil services.

4. An annual membership conference of the corps would be held for, say, three days, and the corps would pay the costs of attendance for members.

5. After not less than fifteen years total of public service and at least five years in the corps, junior members could be nominated for senior membership. Senior members would receive a still higher stipend under the same condition as junior members. They also would elect candidate members, junior members, and senior members.

6. The total number of people in any one corps would eventually be about 500, so that its membership would always be quite select and elite.

7. These grand corps would be fully autonomous, African-controlled bodies. The initial group of senior members would be composed of a dozen Africans who were selected for their exceptional professionalism by a relevant international professional organization. They would select the other members and establish the governance structure of the corps.

8. Each corps would be internationally financed, perhaps by a consortium or the World Bank. The justification for this finance would be

that keeping these professionals in their own countries would have both direct effects on developmental performance and indirect effects on other civil servants that would have a higher rate of return than most donor projects.

9. It is expected that at any given moment, some of these grand corps professionals would be out of favor with their political leaders and therefore might be serving internationally. The corps scheme, however, would produce higher standards of service among those professionals who remained and would facilitate the return to national service of professionals, if and when they returned to political favor.

10. The purpose is *not* to impose international professional policies on national political leaders. It is presumed and would be encouraged that within the bounds of professionalism, there would be substantial differences in the policy views of those elected to membership in a corps. Instead, the intention is to provide a national political leader with the ability to choose among a *range* of dedicated professionals, leading to the selection of ones who simultaneously inspire political confidence, have high competence, and have sufficient autonomy to be able to channel the energy and direction of political will into professional forms that will more likely serve the collective interests of the country.

Notes

Preface

1. Conrad first published the expression, "heart of darkness," in 1899 (in *Blackwood's Magazine*). See Joseph Conrad, *The Heart of Darkness*, edited by Robert Kimbrough, 3rd ed. (New York: W. W. Norton, 1998). The true darkness in the novel was not in Africa or its cultures but in the heart of the European protagonist, who was separated from the controls of his own society. But the image has stuck to Africa itself.

2. Before independence, German colonial authorities carried out a genocide against the Herero of what was then South West Africa and is now Namibia, roughly between 1904 and 1907. Some also contend that the state-orchestrated killing of as many 200,000 Hutu in Burundi in 1972 constituted genocide; see Leo Kuper, *Genocide: Its Political Use in the Twentieth Century* (New Haven: Yale University Press, 1981); and René Lemarchand, *Burundi: Ethnic Conflict and Genocide* (Cambridge: Cambridge University Press, 1994).

3. For us, a system is a patterned set of relationships between actors. It can have effects although it does not have agency, for a system need be nothing more than the norms and regularities that underlie the patterns. For us, then, the "international system" is analogous to a "market."

Chapter 1

1. See Paul Collier and Jan Willem Gunning, "Why Has Africa Grown Slowly?" *Journal of Economic Perspectives* 13, no. 3 (1999): 3–22.

2. Two noteworthy examples are Alec Russell, *Big Men, Little People: The Leaders Who Defined Africa* (New York: New York University Press, 2000); and Blaine Harden, *Africa: Dispatches from a Fragile Continent* (Boston: Houghton Mifflin, 1991).

3. Robert Jackson and Carl Rosberg, *Personal Rule in Black Africa: Prince, Autocrat, Prophet, Tyrant* (Berkeley: University of California Press, 1982).

4. See Michael Bratton and Nicolas van de Walle, *Democratic Experiments in Africa: Regime Transitions in Comparative Perspective* (New York: Cambridge University Press, 1997); William Reno, *Warlord Politics and African States* (Boulder: Lynne Rienner Publishers, 1998); Patrick Chabal and Jean-Pascal Daloz, *Africa Works: Disorder as Political Instrument* (Oxford and Bloomington: James Currey/Indiana University Press, 1999); and Paul Richards, *Fighting for the Rain Forest: War, Youth and Resources in Sierra Leone* (Oxford and Portsmouth, N.H.: James Currey/Heinemann, 1996). The terms of choice in these works tend to be "patrimonialism" or "neopatrimonialism"; these terms are key to these studies, even though the concepts are not the chief concerns of these works. Seen in conjunction with earlier works in which these concepts also are fundamental, we take this as evidence of the centrality of the "personal rule paradigm" to the current understanding and analysis of African politics.

5. "Prebendalism" and "sultanism" are both subtypes of patrimonialism as specified by Weber. For an example of the first, see Richard Joseph, *Democracy and Prebendal Politics in Nigeria* (Cambridge: Cambridge University Press, 1987); for the second, see Richard Sandbrook, with Judith Barker, *The Politics of Africa's Economic Stagnation* (Cambridge: Cambridge University Press, 1985).

6. Max Weber, *Economy and Society*, edited by G. Roth and C. Wittich (Berkeley: University of California Press, 1978), vol. 1, p. 231ff.

7. For extended statements on patrimonialism, see Guenther Roth, "Personal Rulership, Patrimonialism, and Empire-Building in New States," *World Politics* 20, no. 2 (1968): 194–206; and Robin Theobald, "Patrimonialism," *World Politics* 34, no. 4 (1982): 548–559.

8. Jackson and Rosberg, *Personal Rule*.

9. Jean-Francois Médard, "The Underdeveloped State in Tropical Africa: Political Clientelism or Neo-Patrimonialism?" in *Private Patronage and Public Power: Political Clientelism in the Modern State,* edited by Christopher Clapham (New York: St. Martin's Press, 1982); Bratton and van de Walle, *Democratic Experiments*.

10. The concept of weak states refers to the limited degree of state capacity in the following domains: gaining compliance, mobilizing populations, and possessing legitimacy. This definition follows from indicators developed in Joel Migdal, *Strong Societies and Weak States: State-Society Relations and State Capabilities in the Third World* (Princeton: Princeton University Press, 1988), pp. 32–33.

11. Peter Ekeh, "Colonialism and the Two Publics in Africa," *Comparative Studies in Society and History* 17, no. 1 (January 1975): 91–112.

12. The "eating" metaphor is a euphemism for private gain or corruption and is here borrowed from Médard, "The Underdeveloped State," and Jean-Francois Bayart, who aptly characterizes African politics as the "politics of the belly." For the latter, see Bayart, *L'État en Afrique: La Politique du Ventre* (Paris: Fayard, 1989).

13. For an early statement on state collapse, see I. William Zartman, ed., *Collapsed States: The Disintegration and Restoration of Legitimate Authority* (Boulder: Lynne Rienner, 1995). For statements on the relationship between patrimonial politics and state collapse, see Reno, *Warlord Politics,* and Einer Braathen, Morten Bøås, and Gjermund Sæther, *Ethnicity Kills? The Politics of War, Peace, and Ethnicity in Sub-Saharan Africa* (New York: St. Martin's Press, 2000).

14. Cf. Jennifer Widner, *Building the Rule of Law* (New York: W. W. Norton, 2001); David K. Leonard, *African Successes* (Berkeley: University of California Press, 1991).

15. Sandbrook, *The Politics of Africa's Economic Stagnation;* Nicholas van de Walle, *African Economies and the Politics of Permanent Crisis, 1979–1999* (Cambridge: Cambridge University Press, 2001). A review of the literature making this point is provided by Peter Lewis, "Economic Reform and Political Transition in Africa: The Quest for a Politics of Development," *World Politics* 49, no. 1 (1996): 92–129.

16. See Collier and Gunning, "Why Has Africa Grown Slowly?"

17. On this point, see Thomas Callaghy, "The State and the Development of Capitalism in Africa: Theoretical, Historical, and Comparative Reflections," in *The Precarious Balance: State and Society in Africa,* edited by Donald Rothchild and Naomi Chazan (Boulder: Westview Press, 1988).

18. See Benno Ndulu and Stephen O'Connell, "Governance and Growth in Sub-Saharan Africa," *Journal of Economic Perspectives* 13, no. 3 (1999): 41–66.

19. See Goran Hyden, *Beyond Ujamaa in Tanzania* (Berkeley: University of California Press, 1980); and Hyden, *No Shortcuts to Progress: African Development Management in Perspective* (Berkeley: University of California Press, 1983).

20. Chabal and Daloz, *Africa Works.*

21. Frederic Schaffer, *Democracy in Translation: Understanding Politics in an Unfamiliar Culture* (Ithaca: Cornell University Press, 1998).

22. The analysis developed here applies to most of Africa south of the Sahara desert. The conditions in the Republic of South Africa are significantly different, however, and would require a different analysis.

23. Liberia was never technically a colony. It was created by the United States for the benefit of ex-slaves returning to Africa. In this sense, it too was a product of colonialism, enforced by an external white power.

24. For some general discussions on the transcontinental slave trade and its impacts, see Joseph E. Inikori, "Africa in World History: The Export Slave Trade from Africa and the Emergence of the Atlantic Economic Order," in *General History of Africa,* vol. 5, *Africa from the Sixteenth to the Eighteenth Century,* edited by B. A. Ogot (Paris: UNESCO, 1992), pp. 99–110; Joseph E. Inikori, "Slave Trade: Western Africa," in *Encyclopedia of Africa South of the Sahara,* edited by John Middleton, vol. 4 (New York: Scribner's, 1997), pp. 92–93; Roland Oliver and J. D. Fage, *A Short History of Africa* (Baltimore: Penguin Books, 1966), pp. 125–134; John Thornton, *Africa and Africans in the Making of the Atlantic World, 1400–1800,* 2nd ed. (Cambridge: Cambridge University Press, 1998); and Richard Roberts, *Warriors, Merchants, and Slaves* (Stanford: Stanford University Press, 1987). We are particularly grateful to Richard Roberts, professor of African history at Stanford University, for his assistance on this issue.

25. Crawford Young, *The African Colonial State in Comparative Perspective* (New Haven: Yale University Press, 1994).

26. Mahmood Mamdani, *Citizen and Subject: Contemporary Africa and the Legacy of Late Colonialism* (Princeton: Princeton University Press, 1996).

27. Sara Berry, *No Condition Is Permanent: The Social Dynamics of Agrarian Change in Sub-Saharan Africa* (Madison: University of Wisconsin Press, 1993). See also Bruce Berman, "Ethnicity, Patronage, and the African State: The Politics of Uncivil Nationalism," *African Affairs* 97, no. 388 (1998): 305–341; and Berman's critique of Young's thesis, "The Perils of Bula Matari: Constraint and Power in the Colonial State," *Canadian Journal of African Studies* 31, no. 2 (1997): 556–570.

28. In addition to Berry and Berman, for this picture of Africa's colonial experience, see Migdal, *Strong Societies and Weak States.*

29. On the urban biases of African economic policies, see Robert Bates, *States and Markets in Tropical Africa: The Political Basis of Agricultural Policies* (Berkeley: University of California Press, 1981).

30. Robert Jackson and Carl Rosberg, "Why Africa's Weak States Persist: The Empirical and the Juridical in Statehood," *World Politics* 35, no. 1 (1982): 1–24.

31. Weber, *Economy and Society,* vol. 1, pp. 56, 65.

32. See Jackson and Rosberg, "Why Africa's Weak States Persist."

33. The term "quasi-state" is developed in Robert Jackson, *Quasi-States: Sovereignty, International Relations, and the Third World* (Cambridge: Cambridge University Press, 1990).

34. See Nicolas van de Walle and Timothy Johnston, *Improving Aid to Africa* (Baltimore: Johns Hopkins University Press, 1996), p. 20.

35. According to the latest World Bank *World Development Report,* sub-Saharan African countries averaged an ODA level of 9.9 percent of GNP in 1990; the next highest recipient region, the Middle East and North Africa, received 2.1 percent of GNP, and South Asia received 1.5 percent. In 1998, the comparable statistics were 4.1 percent for sub-Saharan Africa, 1 percent for the Middle East and North Africa, and 0.9 percent for South Asia. World Bank,

World Development Report 2000/2001 (New York: Oxford University Press, 2001), table 21.

36. For these statistics, see Shantayanan Devarajan, David Dollar, and Torgny Holmgren, eds., *Aid and Reform in Africa: Lessons from Ten Case Studies* (Washington, D.C.: World Bank, 2000), chap. 1.

37. World Bank, *World Development Report 2000/2001*, Table 21.

38. Reno, *Warlord Politics*.

39. The data for really good quantitative measures of "enclaveness" on the continent do not exist. No statistics exist on key components of the concept. Figures on the inequalities in landownership or income would be partial indicators, but even these data are incomplete for Africa. Further research would be beneficial. Nonetheless, a rough set of indicators and proofs for the argument as it relates to civil conflict is provided in Chapter 4.

40. Donal Cruise O'Brien, *Saints and Politicians: Essays in the Organization of a Senegalese Peasant Society* (London: Cambridge University Press, 1975).

41. A variant of this argument is provided by Robert Bates in *States and Markets*.

42. Paul Collier, "Economic Causes of Civil Conflict and Their Implications for Policy," in *Turbulent Peace,* edited by Chester A. Crocker, Fen Osler Hampson, and Pamela Aall (Washington, D.C.: U.S. Institute of Peace, 2001); Paul Collier and Anke Hoeffler, "On the Economic Causes of Civil War," *Oxford Economic Papers—New Series* 50, no. 4 (1998): 563–573; Paul Collier and Anke Hoeffler, *On the Incidence of Civil War in Africa* (Washington, D.C.: World Bank, August 16, 2000); Ibrahim Elbadawi and Nicholas Sambanis, "Why Are There So Many Civil Wars in Africa? Understanding and Preventing Violent Conflict," *Journal of African Economies* 9, no. 3 (December 2000): 244–269.

43. J. D. Sachs and M. Werner, "Sources of Slow Growth in African Economies," *Journal of African Economies* 6, no. 3 (1997): 335–376. However, the published work of Collier and Gunning at first appears to contradict such an association (see Paul Collier and Jan Gunning, "Explaining African Economic Performance," *Journal of Economic Literature* 37, no. 1 [1999]: table 1). They even argue that Africa's dependence on commodity markets has not damaged its economic performance (Collier and Gunning, "Why Has Africa Grown Slowly?"). Their point, however, is that primary product exports are not negative, *all other things being equal.* And of course, they are not. They have controlled for poor economic policies. Our contention, following on Bates (*States and Markets*) and indeed consistent with Collier's own work on product market policies ("Explaining African Economic Performance") and civil conflict, is that these poor policies themselves are fostered by enclave-dependent economies. Export of primary products is not damaging in itself and indeed is often valuable. It is negative because of its effects on politics and the policies it produces. *Once one controls for these policies,* one would not expect to see a negative association between enclave dependence and economic growth. The task we have set ourselves here is to explore how the damaging

effects of primary product exports on politics can be broken without discontinuing the exports themselves.

44. James D. Fearon and David D. Laitin, "Ethnicity, Insurgency, and Civil War," paper presented to the annual meeting of the American Political Science Association, San Francisco, August 30–September 2, 2001, pp. 23, 25.

45. For a first cut on these issues, see Bates, *States and Markets.* For an economic analysis, see Margaret McMillan and William A. Masters, "A Political Economy Model of Agricultural Taxation, R&D and Growth in Africa," Discussion Paper 99-03, Department of Economics, Tufts University, January 1999.

46. Oliver Williamson, *The Economic Institutions of Capitalism: Firms, Markets and Relational Contracting* (New York: Free Press, 1985).

47. The susceptibility to predation created by asset specificity also has important implications for investor behavior—if predation has ever occurred, investors will assume that it will again and will factor that calculation into any capital put into dedicated assets. That helps explain the resistance of foreign investors to African markets that appear quite profitable. Nonstandard economic policies are needed to deal with this problem, an issue to which we will return in Chapter 2. Ghanaian cocoa producers, who were long subject to similar predation, also have been unwilling to risk being burned again, despite much better cocoa prices from the state. See Lauren Morris MacLean, "Solidarity in Crisis: Social Policies and Social Support Networks in Ghana and Côte d'Ivoire," Ph.D. diss., Department of Political Science, University of California at Berkeley, 2002).

48. Thomas Tomich, Peter Kilby, and Bruce Johnston, *Transforming Agrarian Economies* (Ithaca: Cornell University Press, 1995).

49. Note that none of these points rely on whether the capitalist owner of the enclave is foreign or domestic—this is not an argument about the negative effects of dependence on investments from the metropole. The issue is the form and concentration of the production itself.

50. Terry Lynn Karl, *The Paradox of Plenty: Oil Booms and Petro-States* (Berkeley: University of California Press, 1997), pp. 197–208.

51. Leonard, *African Successes,* chap. 13.

52. Again, the general argument advanced here is very close to and supported by the analysis of unimodal versus bimodal production systems by Tomich, Kilby, and Johnston, *Transforming Agrarian Economies.*

53. These observations rely on private communications with Professor Dennis Galvan, University of Oregon, and Professor Fred Schaffer, Massachusetts Institute of Technology.

Chapter 2

1. These calculations (thirty-three African countries out of forty-one HIPC countries, and two African countries with sustainable levels of debt) are based

on the World Bank's grouping of HIPC countries; see the World Bank HIPC website at http://www.worldbank.org/hipc/Grouping_Final.xls.

2. For *all* of sub-Saharan Africa (including South Africa, which is in relatively good shape), the average debt-to-export ratio in 1995 was 270 percent, and the debt-to-GNP ratio was 74 percent. In 1975, these respective ratios were 51 and 14 percent! See S. Ibi Ajayi and Mohsin S. Khan, eds., *External Debt and Capital Flight in Sub-Saharan Africa* (Washington, D.C.: International Monetary Fund, 2000), pp. 1–2.

3. Cohen holds that countries should devote *no more* than 15 percent of their exports to debt service. But this level is deceptive if applied mechanically to Africa. As we will see, "export income" in Africa includes unusually large amounts of aid, and the loans on which debt service is being paid generally have concessional (i.e., low) interest rates. The 15 percent level of debt service is "sustainable," therefore, only as long as the same levels of aid and concessionality continue. If one wishes to break these chains of dependence and create developmental incentives, as we do, these levels of debt are not repayable. D. Cohen, "The Management of the Developing Countries' Debt: Guidelines and Application to Brazil," *World Bank Economic Review* 2, no. 1 (1988).

4. Even though ODA for sub-Saharan Africa declined from 9.9 percent of GNP in 1990 to 4.1 percent in 1998, the latter figure is still four times that of any other region of the world. World Bank, *World Development Report, 2000–2001* (New York: Oxford University Press, 2001), p. 315.

5. Vinod K. Aggarwal, *Debt Games: Strategic Interaction in International Debt Rescheduling* (New York: Cambridge University Press, 1996), p. 372.

6. Barry Eichengreen, "Historical Research on International Lending and Debt," *Journal of Economic Perspectives* 5, no. 2 (1991): 164.

7. Aggarwal, *Debt Games,* pp. 35, 519, 520. See also Eichengreen, "Historical Research on International Lending and Debt."

8. World Bank, *World Development Report, 2000–2001,* p. 315, table 21.

9. Kathie Krumm, *The External Debt of Sub-Saharan Africa: Origins, Magnitude, and Implications for Action,* World Bank Working Paper No. 741 (Washington, D.C.: World Bank, 1985), p. 2.

10. Ibid., pp. 6–18.

11. Aggarwal, *Debt Games*, pp. 34, 38.

12. World Bank, *Can Africa Claim the 21st Century?* (Washington, D.C.: World Bank, 2000), pp. 21–22.

13. World Bank, *World Development Report, 2000–2001*, pp. 296–297, 312–315.

14. World Bank, *Accelerated Development in Sub-Saharan Africa: An Agenda for Action* (Washington, D.C.: World Bank, 1981).

15. World Bank, *Can Africa Claim the 21st Century?,* chap. 8.

16. Nicolas van de Walle disagrees that Bank aid hastened adjustment in the 1980s. He believes it staved off disaster for a time and thus postponed

reform. Van de Walle, *African Economies and the Politics of Permanent Crisis* (Cambridge: Cambridge University Press, 2001), p. 213.

17. Economic Commission for Africa, *African Alternative Framework to Structural Adjustment Programmes for Socio-economic Recovery and Transformation* (Addis Ababa: United Nations, Economic Commission for Africa, 1989); Sayre Schatz, "Structural Adjustment in Africa: A Failing Grade So Far," *Journal of Modern African Studies* 32, no. 4 (1994): 679–693, and "The World Bank's Fundamental Misconception in Africa," *Journal of Modern African Studies* 34, no. 2 (1996): 239–248. Note the support of both for these particular policies despite their general criticism of structural adjustment.

18. James D. Wolfensohn, "The Other Crisis," Address to the Board of Governors, World Bank, October 6, 1998. World Bank world development reports also assign a positive role to the state; see, for example, World Bank, *World Development Report, 1997: The State in a Changing World* (Washington, D.C.: World Bank, 1997).

19. Paul Collier and Jan Gunning, "Explaining African Economic Performance," *Journal of Economic Literature* 37, no. 1 (1999): table 1.

20. Dani Rodrik, "Development Strategies for the Next Century," paper presented at the conference on "Developing Economies in the Twenty-first Century," Institute for Developing Economies, Japan External Trade Organization, January 26–27, 2000, in Chiba, Japan.

21. Collier and Gunning, "Explaining African Economic Performance."

22. See Shantayanan Devarajan, David Dollar, and Torgny Holmgren, eds., *Aid and Reform in Africa: Lessons from Ten Case Studies* (Washington, D.C.: World Bank, 2000), p. 2: "That the 10 countries in our study all have received large amounts of aid, including conditional loans, yet ended up with vastly different policies, suggests that aid is not a primary determinant of policy." See also Paul Collier and Jan Willem Gunning, "Why Has Africa Grown Slowly?" *Journal of Economic Perspectives* 13, no. 3 (1999): 3–22; and David Dollar and Jakob Svensson, "What Explains the Success or Failure of Structural Adjustment Programs?" *Economic Journal* 110, no. 466 (2000): 894–917.

23. Collier and Gunning, "Explaining African Economic Performance."

24. The same case is made by Carol Lancaster, *Aid to Africa: So Much to Do, So Little Done* (Chicago: University of Chicago Press, 1999), p. 69.

25. Shantayanan Devarajan, Andrew S. Rajkumar, and Vinaya Swaroop, "What Does Aid to Africa Finance?" Framework paper prepared for AERC/ODC Project on Managing a Smooth Transition from Aid Dependence in Africa, October 1998, Washington, D.C., mimeo, as quoted in Carol Lancaster and Samuel Wangwe, *Managing a Smooth Transition from Aid Dependence in Africa* (Baltimore: Johns Hopkins University Press, 2000), p. 16.

26. Van de Walle, *African Economies,* chap. 5.

27. Collier and Gunning, "Explaining African Economic Performance."

28. Our calculations are based on a comparison of tax revenue to overseas development assistance as a percentage of gross national product averaged for 1990 and 1998, as reported in the *World Development Report.* Eleven African

countries, including South Africa, had higher tax revenues than ODA in 1990 and 1998; seven countries reported higher levels of ODA than tax revenues, including Burkina Faso, Burundi, Ethiopia, Madagascar, Malawi, Rwanda, and Sierra Leone. However, numerous countries are without entry for either ODA or tax revenue. Many, such as Zambia, have high ODA levels; others, such as Tanzania, have low tax receipts.

29. See, for example, Alex de Waal, *Famine Crimes: Politics and the Disaster Relief Industry in Africa* (Bloomington: James Currey/Indiana University Press, 1997); and David Keen, *The Benefits of Famine: A Political Economy of Famine in South-Western Sudan, 1983–1989* (Princeton: Princeton University Press, 1994).

30. World Bank, *Assessing Aid: What Works, What Doesn't, and Why* (Washington, D.C.: World Bank, 1998); Devarajan, Dollar, and Holmgren, *Aid and Reform in Africa;* and Lancaster and Wangwe, *Managing a Smooth Transition.* For further references to recent scholarship on aid, see Craig Burnside and David Dollar, "Aid, Policies, and Growth," *American Economic Review* 90, no. 4 (2000): 847–869.

31. Deborah Brautigam, *Aid Dependence and Governance* (Stockholm: Almqvist and Wiksell International, 2000), http://www.ids.ac.uk/eldis/EGDI.htm.

32. According to the 2000/2001 World Bank *World Development Report,* the average sub-Saharan African country received upward of four times as much official development assistance as any other world region. In 1990, sub-Saharan African countries averaged an ODA level of 9.9 percent of GNP; the next highest recipient region, the Middle East and North Africa, received 2.1 percent of GNP, and South Asia received 1.5 percent. In 1998, the comparable statistics were 4.1 percent for sub-Saharan Africa, 1 percent for the Middle East and North Africa, and 0.9 percent for South Asia.

33. Exact time periods are not specified in World Bank documents. Rather, the Bank states that qualifying countries must have "sustained implementation of integrated poverty reduction and economic reform programs." See http://www.worldbank.org/hipc/about/hipcbr/hipcbr.htm.

34. See http://www.jubilee2000uk.org/main.html: "For every $1 received in aid grants in 1999, Sub-Saharan Africa paid back $1.51 in debt service."

35. Ndulu and van de Walle suggest that 20–85 percent of bilateral aid in Africa goes for technical assistance, which is spent on donor-country nationals. Benno Ndulu and Nicolas van de Walle, *Agenda for Africa's Economic Renewal* (New Brunswick: Transaction Publishers, 1996), p. 11. Lancaster and Wangwe report that half of all ODA is recycled into debt payments (*Managing a Smooth Transition,* p. 16). The two studies together make the Jubilee 2000 assertion highly plausible.

36. Lancaster and Wangwe, *Managing a Smooth Transition,* pp. 36–41.

37. Ibrahim Elbadawi, a Sudanese national at the World Bank, argues for precisely such a trade-off. Elbadawi, "Consolidating Macroeconomic Stabi-

lization and Restoring Growth in Africa," in Ndulu and van de Walle, *Agenda for Africa's Economic Renewal*, p. 35.

38. Van de Walle, *African Economies*, pp. 216, 229.

39. There is some international movement toward Goran Hyden's model of politically autonomous development funds. By moving more responsibility for development from international to local actors, this modality would promote the greater autonomy we seek and be a good vehicle for the aid we consider to still be necessary after debt relief. Hyden's proposal is not a substitute for debt relief and a reduction in aid, however. As long as aid is an overwhelming force in African economies, strategies for obtaining it will dominate the calculations of local elites, no matter how it is administered, and weaken their reliance on the productivity of their own population. See Peter H. Koehn and Olatunde J. B. Ojo, eds., *Making Aid Work: Innovative Approaches for Africa at the Turn of the Century* (Lanham, Md.: University Press of America, 1999), part 1.

40. For example, some argue that canceling debt and reducing foreign aid would squander an opportunity to promote democracy and good governance on the continent. Debt relief should be matched with strict conditionality for more accountable government practices. This argument is put forward by Larry Diamond, "Developing Democracy in Africa: African and International Imperatives," *Cambridge Review of International Affairs* 14, no. 1 (2001): 191–213. However, we would argue, first, that current debts and aid dependence do not lead to accountability. Both debt and aid force African elites to be accountable to the international system, not to domestic populations. Second, conditionality has not had a positive effect in Africa and may have had a negative effect.

41. Aggarwal, *Debt Games*, pp. 284–285.

Chapter 3

1. Witness, for example, the widespread support for the efforts of the African Capacity Building Foundation and other similar efforts.

2. Moses Kiggundu, "The Challenges of Management Development in Sub-Saharan Africa," *Journal of Management Development* 10, no. 6 (1991): 42–57. See also Peter Blunt and Merrick L. Jones, *Managing Organizations in Africa* (Berlin: Walter de Gruyter, 1992), pp. 311ff.

3. This section draws heavily on David K. Leonard, *African Successes: Four Public Managers of Kenyan Rural Development* (Berkeley: University of California Press, 1991), chap. 12.

4. John M. Cohen, "Expatriate Advisors in the Government of Kenya: Why They Are There and What Can Be Done About It," Development Discussion Paper No. 376 (Cambridge: Harvard Institute for International Development, 1991); and Cohen, "Foreign Advisors and Capacity Building: The Case of Kenya," *Public Administration and Development* 12 (1992): 493–510.

5. Barbara Grosh, *Public Enterprise in Kenya: What Works, What Doesn't, and Why* (Boulder: Lynne Rienner Publishers, 1991).

6. Rwekaza Mukandala, *The Political Economy of Parastatal Enterprise in Tanzania and Botswana*, Ph.D. diss. (Berkeley: Department of Political Science, University of California, 1988).

7. Philip Selznick, *Leadership in Administration* (New York: Harper and Row, 1957). pp. 7, 57, 59, 62, 66.

8. Chester Barnard, *The Functions of the Executive* (Cambridge: Harvard University Press, 1958), p. 87.

9. Peter B. Vaill, "The Purposing of High-Performing Systems," in *Leadership and Organizational Culture: New Perspectives on Administrative Theory and Practice*, edited by Thomas J. Sergiovanni and John E. Corbally (Urbana: University of Illinois Press, 1984), pp. 91, 93–94; Warren Bennis, "Transformative Power and Leadership," in *Leadership and Organizational Culture*, p. 66; Bennis, *The Chief* (New York: Morrow, 1983).

10. In fact, the author's research has found effective managers in Africa to have *all* the attributes of effective chief executives found by Bennis and Vaill in the United States. See the preceding note.

11. Leonard, *African Successes*, chap. 12.

12. Grosh, *Public Enterprise in Kenya;* Mukandala, *The Political Economy of Parastatal Enterprise in Tanzania and Botswana.*

13. John D. Montgomery, "Bureaucratic Politics in Southern Africa," *Public Administration Review* 46, no. 5 (1986): 411; John D. Montgomery, "Probing Managerial Behavior: Image and Reality in Southern Africa," *World Development* 15, no. 7 (1987): 917, 920.

14. Robert Price, *Society and Bureaucracy in Contemporary Ghana* (Berkeley: University of California Press, 1975).

15. The author owes this point to Norman Uphoff, who has observed the same phenomenon in Sri Lanka.

16. Montgomery, "Bureaucratic Politics in Southern Africa," pp. 411–412.

17. Training in business administration imparts values, but its profit motive too easily reinforces the pursuit of self-interest. Public administration is insufficiently professionalized as a discipline to impart a reliable value content.

18. Cohen, "Expatriate Advisors in the Government of Kenya," p. 14.

19. Ibid., p. 12.

20. Blunt and Jones, *Managing Organizations in Africa*, p. 321.

21. Some technical assistance personnel are quite good at managing staff for professional development, for they are often evaluated on and rewarded for this ability. Their ability to get results has often been inhibited by the absence of a supportive organizational culture and set of incentives for local staff. Cohen, "Expatriate Advisors in the Government of Kenya," pp. 12–13.

22. Moses N. Kiggundu, *Managing Organizations in Developing Countries: An Operational and Strategic Approach* (West Hartford, Conn.: Kumarian Press, 1989), p. 148.

23. Carol Lancaster and Samuel M. Wangwe, *Managing a Smooth Transition from Aid and Dependence in Africa* (Baltimore: Johns Hopkins University Press), p. 44.

24. Elliot J. Berg, Coordinator, *Rethinking Technical Cooperation: Reforms for Capacity Building in Africa* (New York: United Nations Development Programme, 1993).

25. Robert Daland, *Exploring Brazilian Bureaucracy: Performance and Pathology* (Washington, D.C.: University Press of America, 1981); Wolfram Fischer and Peter Lundgreen, "The Recruitment and Training of Administrative and Technical Personnel," in *The Formation of National States in Western Europe*, edited by Charles Tilly (Princeton: Princeton University Press, 1975), pp. 527–543; Leonard White, *The Jacksonians: A Study in Administrative History: 1829–1861* (New York: Macmillan, 1954), pp. 16, 349, 352–353, 357.

Chapter 4

1. A list of civil conflicts can be found later in the chapter. For a reference to Africa's high rates of civil conflict, see Paul Collier and Anke Hoeffler, *On the Incidence of Civil War in Africa* (Washington, D.C.: World Bank, August 16, 2000).

2. For some recent examples of works that explicitly refute the "primordialism" or "tribalism" argument, see Paul Richards, *Fighting for the Rain Forest: War, Youth, and Resources in Sierra Leone* (Oxford and Portsmouth, N.H.: James Currey/Heinemann, 1996); and Einar Braathen, Morten Bøås, and Gjermund Sæther, eds., *Ethnicity Kills? The Politics of War, Peace, and Ethnicity in Sub-Saharan Africa* (New York: St. Martin's Press, 2000).

3. Sudan's contemporary lines of conflict between northerners and southerners arguably date to the precolonial era.

4. One could argue that the conflicts in Angola, Eritrea-Ethiopia, Nigeria, and Rwanda have preindependence roots.

5. Crawford Young and Thomas Turner, *The Rise and Decline of the Zairian State* (Madison: University of Wisconsin Press, 1984), chap. 5.

6. Recent good overviews of this position, as well as that of primordialism, can be found in John Hutchinson and Anthony D. Smith, *Ethnicity* (Oxford: Oxford University Press, 1996); David Lake and Donald Rothchild, eds., *The International Spread of Ethnic Conflict: Fear, Diffusion, and Escalation* (Princeton: Princeton University Press, 1998); and James D. Fearon and David D. Laitin, "Violence and the Social Construction of Ethnic Identity," *International Organization* 54, no. 4 (2000): 845–877.

7. Donald Horowitz, *Ethnic Groups in Conflict* (Berkeley: University of California Press, 1985).

8. Robert Bates, "Modernization, Ethnic Competition, and the Rationality of Politics in Contemporary Politics," in *State Versus Ethnic Claims: African Policy Dilemmas,* edited by Donald Rothchild and Victor Olorunsola (Boulder:

Westview Press, 1983); Young and Turner, *The Rise and Decline;* see also Robert Melson and Howard Wolpe, "Modernization and the Politics of Communalism: A Theoretical Perspective," *American Political Science Review* 64, no. 4 (1970): 1112–1130.

9. For classic accounts on the social construction of nation-states, see Eugen Weber, *Peasants into Frenchmen: The Modernization of Rural France, 1870–1914* (London: Chatto and Windus, 1979), and Benedict Anderson, *Imagined Communities: Reflections on the Origin and Spread of Nationalism* (London: Verso, 1991).

10. Paul Collier, *Economic Causes of Civil Conflict and Their Implications for Policy* (Washington, D.C.: World Bank, June 15, 2000).

11. Collier and Hoeffler, *On the Incidence of Civil War.*

12. Ibrahim Elbadawi and Nicholas Sambanis, "Why Are There So Many Civil Wars in Africa? Understanding and Preventing Violent Conflict," *Journal of African Economies* 9, no. 3 (2000): 244–269; Michael Doyle and Nicholas Sambanis, "International Peacebuilding: A Theoretical and Quantitative Analysis," *American Political Science Review* 94, no. 4 (2000): 779–801.

13. D. C. Esty, J. A. Goldstone, T. R. Gurr, B. Harff, M. Levy, G. D. Dabelko, P. T. Surko, and A. N. Unger, *State Failure Task Force Report: Phase II Findings* (McLean, Va.: Science Applications International Corporation, July 31, 1998), pp. 15, 30, 9.

14. James Fearon and David Laitin, "Ethnicity, Insurgency, and Civil War," paper presented to the annual meetings of the American Political Science Association, San Francisco, August 30–September 2, 2001.

15. Paul Collier and Anke Hoeffler, *Greed and Grievance in Civil War* (Washington, D.C.: World Bank, January 4, 2001).

16. Lake and Rothchild, *The International Spread of Ethnic Conflict*, is a good example of this.

17. In the early versions of his work, Collier presented his analysis as determining whether conflict is caused by grievances *or* greed and opted for the latter. We do *not* agree with this formulation. More recently, he has argued that the ability to wage a civil war around either grievances or greed depends on the ability of rebels to capture resources to finance their efforts. Doing so often involves predation, especially in Africa. This formulation strikes us as powerful for African conflicts. (We are less certain about those elsewhere, for example, in the formerly Communist states of Eastern Europe and Eurasia.)

18. Collier, *Economic Causes,* p. 4.

19. See Collier and Hoeffler, *On the Incidence of Civil War in Africa.*

20. Collier, *Economic Causes,* p. 6.

21. Ibid.

22. Ibid., p. 17. See also Doyle and Sambanis, "International Peacebuilding."

23. Collier, *Economic Causes,* p. 9.

24. Ibid., pp. 9–10.

25. Collier does suggest that in the rest of the world, a few extremely rich oil exporters have been able to use their resources in a way that avoids this trap. Thus the causal relationship is curvilinear. Collier and Hoeffler, *Greed and Grievance in Civil War.*

26. Collier makes a similar point in his discussion of diasporic networks.

27. We would point out here that coercive capacity is integral to many definitions of states. In *Economy and Society*, for example, Max Weber defines states as having a monopoly on the legitimate use of force. See Weber, *Economy and Society,* edited by G. Roth and C. Wittich (Berkeley: University of California Press, 1978). Joel Migdal also argues that a state's ability to gain compliance is a basic measure of capacity and that compliance often is gained through force. See Migdal, *Strong Societies and Weak States: State-Society Relations and State Capabilities in the Third World* (Princeton: Princeton University Press, 1988), p. 32.

28. In "Ethnicity, Insurgency, and Civil War," Fearon and Laitin argue that the observed cross-national correlation between national poverty and conflict is due to the close relationship of the former to state weakness.

29. We borrow a recent, useful, six-point criterion for determining whether a country has or does not have civil conflict: whether conflict (1) caused more than 1,000 deaths in at least a single year; (2) challenged the sovereignty of an internationally recognized state; (3) occurred within the recognized boundary of that state; (4) involved the state as a major combatant; and (5) included rebels with the ability to mount organized armed opposition to the state; and whether (6) the parties would live together in the same political unit at war's end. See Doyle and Sambanis, "International Peacebuilding."

30. This information and other statistical information is drawn from the latest Economist Intelligence Unit's *Country Profiles* and *Country Reports*, the World Bank's *World Development Report*, and the CIA's *World Factbook.*

31. See Global Witness's 1998 report, *A Rough Trade: The Role of Companies and Governments in the Angolan Conflict.* The report can be found on the Internet at http://www.oneworld.org/globalwitness/reports/Angola/cover. htm.

32. For an excellent account of the Angolan civil war and this conflict's dependence on oil and diamonds, see Tony Hodges, *Angola: From Afro-Stalinism to Petro-Diamond Capitalism* (Oxford: James Currey, 2001).

33. See Global Witness, *Conflict Diamonds: Possibilities for the Identification, Certification and Control of Diamonds,* http://www.oneworld.org/ globalwitness/reports/conflict/conflict.htm, June 2000.

34. David J. Gould, *Bureaucratic Corruption and Underdevelopment in the Third World: The Case of Zaire* (New York: Pergamon Press, 1980).

35. Global Witness, "Zimbabwe's Resource Colonialism in the DRC," http://www.oneworld.org/globalwitness/press/bd_zimbabwe.htm.

36. For a damning report on Uganda's and Rwanda's resource exploitation in the Democratic Republic of Congo, see United Nations, "Report on the Panel of Experts on the Illegal Exploitation of Natural Resources and Other

Forms of Wealth of the Democratic Republic of the Congo," Document S/2001/357, April 2001.

37. For discussions of the connections between resources, personal rule, and conflict in the Democratic Republic of Congo, as well as in Liberia, Sierra Leone, and Nigeria, see William Reno, *Warlord Politics and African States* (Boulder: Lynne Rienner Publishers, 1998).

38. United Nations, "Report of the Panel of Experts Appointed Pursuant to UN Security Council 1306 (2000), Paragraph 19 in Relation to Sierra Leone," S/2000/1195, December 20, 2000, paragraph 1.

39. The Economist Intelligence Unit, "Sierra Leone Country Profile" (London: Economist Intelligence Unit, September 8, 2000).

40. For further discussions of resources and the Sierra Leone conflict, see John Hirsch, *Sierra Leone: Diamonds and the Struggle for Democracy* (Boulder: Lynne Rienner Publishers, 2001) and Richards, *Fighting for the Rain Forest.*

41. United Nations, "Report of the Panel of Experts Appointed Pursuant to UN Security Council 1306 (2000)," paragraph 122.

42. Global Witness, "The Role of Liberia's Logging Industry on National and Regional Insecurity," http://www.oneworld.org/globalwitness/press/gwliberia.htm, January 2001.

43. Michael Watts, ed., *State, Oil, and Agriculture in Nigeria* (Berkeley: Institute of International Studies, University of California, 1987).

44. Richard Joseph, "The Reconfiguration of Power in Late Twentieth-Century Africa," in *State, Conflict and Democracy in Africa*, edited by Richard Joseph (Boulder: Lynne Rienner Publishers, 1999), pp. 74–75.

45. Carrie L. Manning, "Democratic Transition in Mozambique, 1992–1995: Beginning at the End?" Ph.D. diss., Department of Political Science, University of California at Berkeley, 1997.

46. Khalid Medani, "Market Crocodiles in an Age of Cannibalism: The Role of the Parallel Market in State Formation and Collapse in Sudan and Somalia," M.A. thesis, Department of Political Science, University of California at Berkeley, 1995.

47. For an excellent analysis of the Rwandan genocide, see Alison Des Forges, *Leave None to the Tell the Story: Genocide in Rwanda* (New York: Human Rights Watch, 1999).

48. John Chipman, *French Power in Africa* (Oxford: Basil Blackwell, 1989); David E. Gardinier, "Gabon: Limited Reform and Regime Survival," in *Political Reform in Francophone Africa*, edited by J. F. Clark and D. E. Gardinier (Boulder: Westview Press, 1997); Michael C. Reed, "Gabon: A Neo-Colonial Enclave of Enduring French Interest," *Journal of Modern African Studies* 25, no. 2 (1987); and Douglas A. Yates, *The Rentier State in Africa: Oil Rent Dependency and Neocolonialism in the Republic of Gabon* (Trenton: Africa World Press, 1996), chap. 3. We are grateful to Sam Angus for the research that led us to these references.

49. Determination of conflict for the African cases under consideration (excepting those that had conflict from a war of independence) is taken from Doyle and Sambanis, "International Peacebuilding." p. 784. At the time, Sambanis was part of the World Bank research team working on civil conflict; on p. 783, footnote 16, of their article, Doyle and Sambanis reference a World Bank website for their coding decisions on conflict. As such, we refer to this scholarship as part of that of the "World Bank group."

50. Obviously it would be preferable to use statistics on the structure of an economy at a time closer to the outbreak of conflict than 1999. The general structure of most African economies has been fairly stable, however, and these statistics give us an adequate rough measure.

51. Fearon and Laitin, "Ethnicity, Insurgency and Civil War." James Fearon was particularly helpful to us in working through and testing our alternate specifications for enclave production and state weakness. Of course, we remain solely responsible for the outcome.

52. Evan S. Lieberman, "Taxation Data as Indicators of State-Society Relations: Possibilities and Pitfalls in Cross-National Research," *Studies in Comparative International Development* 36, no. 4 (2002): 89–115.

Chapter 5

1. Barbara Crossette, "U.N. Chief Wants Faster Action to Avoid Slaughter in Civil Wars," *New York Times,* September 21, 1999, p. A1; David Sanger, "Clinton Warns U.N. of a New Age of Civil Wars." *New York Times*, September 17, 2000, A1; see also Gareth Evans, *Cooperating for Peace: The Global Agenda for the 1990s and Beyond* (Victoria, Australia: Allen and Unwin, 1993).

2. David K. Leonard and Scott Straus, "Humanitarian Intervention in Sub-Saharan Africa," in *New Challenge: "Humanitarian Intervention" in International Relations*, edited by Yang Cheng-xu and Wu Miao-fa (Beijing: China Youth Press, 2000). See also Thomas G. Weiss, "On the Brink of a New Era? Humanitarian Interventions, 1991–1994," in *Beyond Traditional Peacekeeping*, edited by Donald C. F. Daniel and Bradd C. Hayes, eds. (New York: St. Martin's, 1995); John F. Garofano, "An Emerging Norm of Humanitarian Intervention? The Future of the Pretty Good Samaritans," and Rita Parhad and Scott Straus, "An Emerging Norm of Humanitarian Intervention? The Case of Genocide," papers delivered at the 2000 annual meeting of the American Political Science Association (APSA), Washington, D.C., August 31–September 3, 2000; APSA papers available at http://PRO.harvard.edu.

3. See Parhad and Straus, "An Emerging Norm."

4. Sudan is the one exception, for it is thought that a fundamentalist Islamic government there might affect Egypt and therefore the rest of the delicate balance of power in the Middle East.

5. The Nigerian failure in Liberia was partly due to questions about its motives and the genuineness of its regional support. But ECOWAS's formal

sanction was nevertheless obtained. Herbert Howe, "Lessons from Liberia: ECOMOG and Regional Peacekeeping," in *Nationalism and Ethnic Conflict*, edited by M. E. Brown, O. R. Coté, S. M. Lynn-Jones, and S. E. Miller, rev. ed. (Cambridge: MIT Press, 2001), pp. 267–298.

6. Paul Collier, *Economic Causes of Civil Conflict and Their Implications for Policy* (Washington, D.C.: World Bank, June 15, 2000), p. 6.

7. Ibid.

8. These ideas were argued back and forth by the graduate students in a course on African conflicts we cotaught with Donald Rothchild at the University of California at Berkeley in spring 2002. Although the students did not reach consensus on *what* to do, they did agree that the analytics offered here are *how* one has to think about these problems. We are grateful to the class for this contribution to our thinking.

9. D. C. Esty, J. A. Goldstone, T. R. Gurr, B. Harff, M. Levy, G. D. Dabelko, P. T. Surko, and A. N. Unger, *State Failure Task Force Report: Phase II Findings* (McLean, Va.: Science Applications International Corporation, July 31, 1998), pp. 9, 15.

10. James D. Fearon and David D. Laitin, "Ethnicity, Insurgency, and Civil War," paper presented to the annual meeting of the American Political Science Association, San Francisco, August 30–September 2, 2001, pp. 23, 25; David A. Lake and Donald Rothchild, "Containing Fear: The Origins and Management of Ethnic Conflict," in *Nationalism and Ethnic Conflict*, edited by M. E. Brown, O. R. Coté, S. M. Lynn-Jones, and S. E. Miller, rev. ed. (Cambridge, Mass.: MIT Press, 2001), pp. 125–160.

11. A security dilemma is a subtype of the "Prisoners' Dilemma," another common term in the game theory literature. James Fearon, "Rationalist Explanations for War," *International Organization* 49, no. 3 (Summer 1995): 379–414; Fearon, "Ethnic Conflict as a Commitment Problem," unpublished manuscript, 1993 as cited in David A. Lake and Donald Rothchild, "Containing Fear": The Origins and Management of Ethnic Conflict," in *Nationalism and Ethnic Conflict*, edited by M. E. Brown, O. R. Coté, S. M. Lynn-Jones, and S. E. Miller, rev. ed. (Cambridge, Mass.: MIT Press, 2001).

12. John Mueller, "The Banality of 'Ethnic War,'" in *Nationalism and Ethnic Conflict*, edited by M. E. Brown, O. R. Coté, S. M. Lynn-Jones, and S. E. Miller, rev. ed. (Cambridge: MIT Press, 2001), pp. 97–125.

13. James Fearon and David Laitin, "Violence and the Social Construction of Ethnicity," *International Organization* 54, no. 4 (Autumn 2000): 845–877.

14. This causal story does not work as well for the civil wars in the former Communist states, where something different seems to be going on. But in Africa, where interstate boundaries are rarely contested, diaspora groups are too small and poor to finance significant rebellions, and other states have relatively little interest in funding them either, the logic is very powerful. Deliberations of the conference on "The Political Economy of Civil Wars: Implications for Mediation, Peacebuilding and Prevention," Institute for International Studies, Stanford University, August 10–12, 2001.

15. Esty et al., *State Failure Task Force Report: Phase II Findings*, pp. 14, 15; Fearon and Laitin, "Ethnicity, Insurgency and Civil War," p. 22.

16. Richard Joseph, "The Reconfiguration of Power in Late Twentieth-Century Africa," in *State, Conflict, and Democracy in Africa*, edited by Richard Joseph (Boulder: Lynne Rienner Publishers, 1999), pp. 74–75.

17. Paul Collier, *Economic Causes*.

18. For an excellent discussion of these issues, see Adam Przeworski, Michael E. Alvarez, José Antonio Cheibub, and Fernando Limongi, *Democracy and Development: Political Institutions and Well-Being in the World, 1950–1990* (New York: Cambridge University Press, 2000).

19. Ibrahim Elbadawi and Nicholas Sambanis, "Why Are There So Many Civil Wars in Africa? Understanding and Preventing Violent Conflict," *Journal of African Economies* 9, no. 3 (2000): 244–269. They actually argue that democracy reduces the prospects of violent conflict more generally. Paul Collier finds no relationship between democracy and civil conflict, however, and his data set is almost identical to that of Elbadawi and Sambanis. The sole difference in their data sets is that the latter include cases where conflict has occurred in the preceding period and Collier does not. The clear implication is that democracy is highly correlated with success in holding the peace.

20. Esty et al., *State Failure Task Force Report: Phase II Findings*, pp. 9, 15; Fearon and Laitin, "Ethnicity, Insurgency, and Civil War," p. 25.

21. Fearon and Laitin, "Ethnicity, Insurgency, and Civil War," p. 26.

22. John Spanier writes that "an intervention on the side of those less than 100 per cent democratically pure tends to mobilize political opposition, divide the public, and provoke critical world opinion." Spanier, *Games Nations Play*, 8th ed. (Washington, D.C.: Congressional Quarterly, 1993), p. 504.

23. Professor Goran Hyden, University of Florida, private communication.

24. John Chipman, *French Power in Africa* (Oxford: Basil Blackwell, 1989), pp. 128–130.

25. Joseph, "The Reconfiguration of Power," pp. 74–75.

26. See, for example, the overview provided in some of the leading recent texts: Glenn Hastedt and Kay Knickrehm, *Dimensions of World Politics* (New York: HarperCollins, 1991); Bruce Russett and Harvey Staff, *World Politics*, 5th ed. (New York: W. H. Freeman, 1996); and John Spanier, *Games Nations Play*. Also helpful is James D. Fearon, "Signaling Foreign Policy Interests: Tying Hands Versus Sinking Cost," *Journal of Conflict Resolution* 41, no.1 (February 1997): 68–90.

27. Jose Edgardo Campos and Hadi Salehi Esfahani, "Credible Commitment and Success with Public Enterprise Reform," *World Development* 28, no. 2 (2000): 221–243; Thrainn Eggertsson, "Mental Models and Social Values: North's Institutions and Credible Commitment," *Journal of Institutional and Theoretical Economics* 149 (1993): 24–28; Gary Miller, "Confiscation, Credible Commitment, and Progressive Reform in the United States," *Journal of Institutional and Theoretical Economics* 145 (1989): 686–692; Nahalel Nellis,

"Deficiencies in European Monetary Union's Credible Commitment Against Monetary Expansion," *Cornell International Law Journal* 33 (2000): 263–296; Douglass North, "Institutions and Credible Commitment," *Journal of Institutional and Theoretical Economics* 149 (1993): 11–23; and North, *Institutions, Institutional Change, and Economic Performance* (Cambridge: Cambridge University Press, 1990).

28. Russett and Staff, *World Politics,* p. 90.

29. "It appears that the principal prerequisites for future Western interventions are a worthy cause, the assurance of relatively few casualties, and good chances for successfully achieving one's objective in a short period of time." Spanier, *Games Nations Play,* p. 507.

30. Chipman, *French Power in Africa;* Joseph, "The Reconfiguration of Power"; and Sam Angus, unpublished paper, University of California at Berkeley, Department of Political Science, 2002.

31. Joseph, "The Reconfiguration of Power"; Douglas A. Yates, *The Rentier State in Africa: Oil Rent Dependency and Neocolonialism in the Republic of Gabon* (Trenton: Africa World Press, 1996).

32. Kenneth Shepsle, "Discretion, Institutions, and the Problem of Government Commitment," in *Social Theory for a Changing Society,* edited by Pierre Bourdieu and James Coleman (Boulder: Westview Press, 1991).

33. Nellis, "Deficiencies," p. 274.

Appendix B

1. This appendix is reproduced, with minor alterations, from David K. Leonard, "Professionalism and African Administration," *IDS Bulletin* 24, no. 1 (1993): 77–78.

2. Ezra N. Suleiman, *Politics, Power, and Bureaucracy in France: The Administrative Elite* (Princeton: Princeton University Press, 1974); Suleiman, *Elites in French Society: The Politics of Survival* (Princeton: Princeton University Press, 1978).

3. Moses Kiggundu, *Managing Organizations in Developing Countries: An Operational and Strategic Approach* (West Hartford, Conn.: Kumarian Press, 1989), p. 175.

Bibliography

Aggarwal, Vinod K. *Debt Games: Strategic Interaction in International Debt Rescheduling.* New York: Cambridge University Press, 1996.

Anderson, Benedict. *Imagined Communities: Reflections on the Origin and Spread of Nationalism.* London: Verso, 1991.

Barnard, Chester. *The Functions of the Executive.* Cambridge: Harvard University Press, 1958.

Bates, Robert. "Modernization, Ethnic Competition, and the Rationality of Politics in Contemporary Politics." In *State Versus Ethnic Claims: African Policy Dilemmas,* edited by Donald Rothchild and Victor Olorunsola. Boulder: Westview Press, 1983.

————. *States and Markets in Tropical Africa: The Political Basis of Agricultural Policies.* Berkeley: University of California Press, 1981.

Bayart, Jean-Francois. *L'État en Afrique: La Politique du Ventre.* Paris: Fayard, 1989.

Bennis, Warren. *The Chief.* New York: Morrow, 1983.

————. "Transformative Power and Leadership." In *Leadership and Organizational Culture: New Perspectives on Administrative Theory and Practice,* edited by Thomas J. Sergiovanni and John E. Corbally. Urbana: University of Illinois Press, 1984.

Berg, Elliot J. *Rethinking Technical Cooperation: Reforms for Capacity Building in Africa.* New York: United Nations Development Programme, 1993.

Berman, Bruce. "Ethnicity, Patronage, and the African State: The Politics of Uncivil Nationalism." *African Affairs* 97, no. 388 (1998): 305–341.

————. "The Perils of Bula Matari: Constraint and Power in the Colonial State." *Canadian Journal of African Studies* 31, no. 2 (1997): 556–570.

Berry, Sara. *No Condition Is Permanent: The Social Dynamics of Agrarian Change in Sub-Saharan Africa.* Madison: University of Wisconsin Press, 1993.

Blunt, Peter, and Merrick L. Jones. *Managing Organizations in Africa.* Berlin: Walter de Gruyter, 1992.

139

Braathen, Einer, Morten Bøås, and Gjermund Sæther. *Ethnicity Kills? The Politics of War, Peace, and Ethnicity in Sub-Saharan Africa.* New York: St. Martin's Press, 2000.

Bratton, Michael, and Nicolas van de Walle. *Democratic Experiments in Africa: Regime Transitions in Comparative Perspective.* New York: Cambridge University Press, 1997.

Brautigam, Deborah. *Aid Dependence and Governance.* Stockholm: Almqvist and Wiksell International, 2000 See also http://www.ids.ac.uk/eldis/EGDI.htm.

Burnside, Craig, and David Dollar. "Aid, Policies, and Growth." *American Economic Review* 90, no. 4 (2000): 847–869.

Callaghy, Thomas. "The State and the Development of Capitalism in Africa: Theoretical, Historical, and Comparative Reflections." In *The Precarious Balance: State and Society in Africa,* edited by Donald Rothchild and Naomi Chazan. Boulder: Westview Press, 1988.

Campos, Jose Edgardo, and Hadi Salehi Esfahani. "Credible Commitment and Success with Public Enterprise Reform." *World Development* 28, no. 2 (2000): 221–243.

Central Intelligence Agency. *World Factbook.* Washington, D.C.: Central Intelligence Agency, 2000.

Chabal, Patrick, and Jean-Pascal Daloz. *Africa Works: Disorder as Political Instrument.* Oxford and Bloomington: James Currey/Indiana University Press, 1999.

Chipman, John. *French Power in Africa.* Oxford: Basil Blackwell, 1989.

Cohen, D. "The Management of the Developing Countries' Debt: Guidelines and Application to Brazil." *World Bank Economic Review* 2, no. 1 (1988).

Cohen, John M. "Expatriate Advisors in the Government of Kenya: Why They Are There and What Can Be Done About It." Development Discussion Paper No. 376. Cambridge, Mass.: Harvard Institute for International Development, 1991.

———. "Foreign Advisors and Capacity Building: The Case of Kenya." *Public Administration and Development* 12 (1992): 493–510.

Collier, Paul. "Economic Causes of Civil Conflict and Their Implications for Policy." In *Turbulent Peace: The Challenges of Managing International Conflict,* edited by Chester A. Crocker, Fen Osler Hampson, and Pamela Aall. Washington, D.C.: United States Institute of Peace, 2001.

Collier, Paul, and Jan Willem Gunning. "Explaining African Economic Performance." *Journal of Economic Literature* 37, no. 1 (1999): 64-111.

———. "Why Has Africa Grown Slowly?" *Journal of Economic Perspectives* 13, no. 3 (1999): 3–22.

Collier, Paul, and Anke Hoeffler. *Greed and Grievance in Civil War.* Washington, D.C.: World Bank, January 4, 2001.

———. "On the Economic Causes of Civil War." *Oxford Economic Papers—New Series* 50, no. 4 (1998): 563–573.

————. *On the Incidence of Civil War in Africa.* World Bank Working Paper. Washington, D.C.: World Bank, August 16, 2000 Available at http://www.worldbank.org/research/conflict.

Conrad, Joseph. *The Heart of Darkness.* Edited by Robert Kimbrough, 3rd ed. New York: W. W. Norton, 1998.

Crossette, Barbara. "U.N. Chief Wants Faster Action to Avoid Slaughter in Civil Wars." *New York Times,* September 21, 1999, p. A1.

Daland, Robert. *Exploring Brazilian Bureaucracy: Performance and Pathology.* Washington, D.C.: University Press of America, 1981.

Des Forges, Alison. *Leave None to Tell the Story: Genocide in Rwanda.* New York: Human Rights Watch, 1999.

Devarajan, Shantayanan, David Dollar, and Torgny Holmgren, eds. *Aid and Reform in Africa: Lessons from Ten Case Studies.* Washington, D.C.: World Bank, 2000.

de Waal, Alex. *Famine Crimes: Politics and the Disaster Relief Industry in Africa.* Bloomington: James Currey/Indiana University Press, 1997.

Diamond, Larry. "Developing Democracy in Africa: African and International Imperatives." *Cambridge Review of International Affairs* 14, no. 1 (2001): 191–213.

Dollar, David, and Jakob Svensson. "What Explains the Success or Failure of Structural Adjustment Programs?" *Economic Journal* 110, no. 466 (2000): 894–917.

Doyle, Michael, and Nicholas Sambanis. "International Peacebuilding: A Theoretical and Quantitative Analysis." *American Political Science Review* 94, no. 4 (2000): 779–801.

Economic Commission for Africa. *African Alternative Framework to Structural Adjustment Programmes for Socio-economic Recovery and Transformation.* Addis Ababa: United Nations, Economic Commission for Africa, 1989.

Economist Intelligence Unit. "Sierra Leone Country Profile." London: Economic Intelligence Unit, September 8, 2000.

Eggertsson, Thrainn. "Mental Models and Social Values: North's Institutions and Credible Commitment." *Journal of Institutional and Theoretical Economics* 149 (1993): 24–28.

Eichengreen, Barry. "Historical Research on International Lending and Debt." *Journal of Economic Perspectives* 5, no. 2 (1991): 149–169.

Ekeh, Peter. "Colonialism and the Two Publics in Africa." *Comparative Studies in Society and History* 17, no. 1 (January 1975): 91–112.

Elbadawi, Ibrahim. "Consolidating Macroeconomic Stabilization and Restoring Growth in Africa." In *Agenda for Africa's Economic Renewal,* edited by Benno Ndulu and Nicolas van de Walle. New Brunswick: Transaction Publishers, 1996.

Elbadawi, Ibrahim, and Nicholas Sambanis. "Why Are There So Many Civil Wars in Africa? Understanding and Preventing Violent Conflict." *Journal of African Economies* 9, no. 3 (2000): 244–269.

Esty, D. C., J. A. Goldstone, T. R. Gurr, B. Harff, M. Levy, G. D. Dabelko, P. T. Surko, and A. N. Unger. *State Failure Task Force Report: Phase II Findings.* McLean, Va.: Science Applications International Corporation, July 31, 1998.

Evans, Gareth. *Cooperating for Peace: The Global Agenda for the 1990s and Beyond.* St. Leonards, Australia: Allen and Unwin, 1993.

Fearon, James. "Rationalist Explanations for War." *International Organization* 49, no. 3 (Summer 1995): 379–414.

———. "Signaling Foreign Policy Interests: Tying Hands Versus Sinking Cost." *Journal of Conflict Resolution* 41, no. 1 (February 1997): 68–90.

Fearon, James D., and David D. Laitin. "Ethnicity, Insurgency and Civil War." Paper presented to the annual meeting of the American Political Science Association, San Francisco, August 30–September 2, 2001.

———. "Violence and the Social Construction of Ethnic Identity." *International Organization* 54, no. 4 (2000): 845–877.

Fischer, Wolfram, and Peter Lundgreen. "The Recruitment and Training of Administrative and Technical Personnel." In *The Formation of National States in Western Europe,* edited by Charles Tilly. Princeton: Princeton University Press, 1975.

Gardinier, David E. "Gabon: Limited Reform and Regime Survival." In *Political Reform in Francophone Africa,* edited by J. F. Clark and D. E. Gardinier. Boulder: Westview Press, 1997.

Garofano, John F. "An Emerging Norm of Humanitarian Intervention? The Future of the Pretty Good Samaritans." Paper delivered at the annual meeting of the American Political Science Association, Washington, D.C., August 31–September 3, 2000.

Global Witness. *Conflict Diamonds: Possibilities for the Identification, Certification, and Control of Diamonds.* http://www.oneworld.org/globalwitness/reports/conflict/conflict.htm, June 2000.

———. "The Role of Liberia's Logging Industry on National and Regional Insecurity." http://www.oneworld.org/globalwitness/press/gwliberia.htm, January 2001.

———. *A Rough Trade: The Role of Companies and Governments in the Angolan Conflict.* http://www.oneworld.org/globalwitness/reports/Angola/cover.htm, 1998.

———. "Zimbabwe's Resource Colonialism in the DRC." http://www.oneworld.org/globalwitness/press/bd_zimbabwe.htm, n.d.

Gould, David J. *Bureaucratic Corruption and Underdevelopment in the Third World: The Case of Zaire.* New York: Pergamon Press, 1980.

Grosh, Barbara. *Public Enterprise in Kenya: What Works, What Doesn't and Why.* Boulder: Lynne Rienner Publishers, 1991.

Harden, Blaine. *Africa: Dispatches from a Fragile Continent.* Boston: Houghton Mifflin, 1991.

Hastedt, Glen, and Kay Knickrehm. *Dimensions of World Politics.* New York: HarperCollins, 1991.

Hirsch, John. *Sierra Leone: Diamonds and the Struggle for Democracy*. Boulder: Lynne Rienner Publishers, 2001.

Hodges, Tony. *Angola: from Afro-Stalinism to Petro-Diamond Capitalism*. Oxford: James Currey, 2001.

Horowitz, Donald. *Ethnic Groups in Conflict*. Berkeley: University of California Press, 1985.

Howe, Herbert. "Lessons from Liberia: ECOMOG and Regional Peacekeeping." In *Nationalism and Ethnic Conflict,* edited by M. E. Brown, O. R. Coté, S. M. Lynn-Jones, and S. E. Miller. Rev. ed. Cambridge: MIT Press, 2001.

Hutchinson, John, and Anthony D. Smith. *Ethnicity*. Oxford: Oxford University Press, 1996.

Hyden, Goran. *Beyond Ujamaa in Tanzania*. Berkeley: University of California Press, 1980.

———. *No Shortcuts to Progress: African Development Management in Perspective*. Berkeley: University of California Press, 1983.

Ibi Ajayi, S., and Mohsin S. Khan, eds. *External Debt and Capital Flight in Sub-Saharan Africa*. Washington, D.C.: International Monetary Fund, 2000.

Inikori, Joseph E. "Africa in World History: The Export Slave Trade from Africa and the Emergence of the Atlantic Economic Order." In *General History of Africa*. Vol. 5, *Africa from the Sixteenth to the Eighteenth Century*, edited by B. A. Ogot. Paris: UNESCO, 1992.

———. "Slave Trade: Western Africa." In *Encyclopedia of Africa South of the Sahara,* edited by John Middleton, vol. 4. New York: Scribner's, 1997.

Jackson, Robert. *Quasi-States: Sovereignty, International Relations, and the Third World*. Cambridge: Cambridge University Press, 1990.

Jackson, Robert, and Carl Rosberg. *Personal Rule in Black Africa: Prince, Autocrat, Prophet, Tyrant*. Berkeley: University of California Press, 1982.

———. "Why Africa's Weak States Persist: The Empirical and the Juridical in Statehood." *World Politics* 35, no. 1 (1982): 1–24.

Joseph, Richard. *Democracy and Prebendal Politics in Nigeria: The Rise and Fall of the Second Republic*. Cambridge: Cambridge University Press, 1987.

———. "The Reconfiguration of Power in Late Twentieth-Century Africa." In *State, Conflict and Democracy in Africa,* edited by Richard Joseph. Boulder: Lynne Rienner Publishers, 1999.

Karl, Terry Lynn. *The Paradox of Plenty: Oil Booms and Petro-States*. Berkeley: University of California Press, 1997.

Keen, David. *The Benefits of Famine: A Political Economy of Famine in South-Western Sudan, 1983–1989*. Princeton: Princeton University Press, 1994.

Kiggundu, Moses. "The Challenges of Management Development in Sub-Saharan Africa." *Journal of Management Development* 10, no. 6 (1991): 42–57.

———. *Managing Organizations in Developing Countries: An Operational and Strategic Approach.* West Hartford, Conn.: Kumarian Press, 1989.

Koehn, Peter H., and Olatunde J. B. Ojo, eds. *Making Aid Work: Innovative Approaches for Africa at the Turn of the Century.* Lanham, Md.: University Press of America, 1999.

Krumm, Kathie. *The External Debt of Sub-Saharan Africa: Origins, Magnitude, and Implications for Action.* World Bank Working Paper No. 741. Washington, D.C.: World Bank, 1985.

Kuper, Leo. *Genocide: Its Political Use in the Twentieth Century.* New Haven: Yale University Press, 1981.

Lake, David A., and Donald Rothchild. "Containing Fear: The Origins and Management of Ethnic Conflict." In *Nationalism and Ethnic Conflict,* edited by M. E. Brown, O. R. Coté, S. M. Lynn-Jones, and S. E. Miller. Rev. ed. Cambridge, Mass.: MIT Press, 2001.

Lake, David A., and Donald Rothchild, eds. *The International Spread of Ethnic Conflict: Fear, Diffusion, and Escalation.* Princeton: Princeton University Press, 1998.

Lancaster, Carol. *Aid to Africa: So Much to Do, So Little Done.* Chicago: University of Chicago Press, 1999.

Lancaster, Carol, and Samuel M. Wangwe. *Managing a Smooth Transition from Aid Dependence in Africa.* Baltimore: Johns Hopkins University Press, 2000.

Lemarchand, René. *Burundi: Ethnic Conflict and Genocide.* Cambridge: Cambridge University Press, 1994.

Leonard, David K. *African Successes: Four Public Managers of Kenyan Rural Development.* Berkeley: University of California Press, 1991.

———. "Professionalism and African Administration." *IDS Bulletin* 24, no. 1 (1993): 77–78.

Leonard, David K., and Scott Straus. "Humanitarian Intervention in Sub-Saharan Africa." In *New Challenge: "Humanitarian Intervention" in International Relations,* edited by Yang Cheng-xu and Wu Miao-fa. Beijing: China Youth Press, 2000.

Lewis, Peter. "Economic Reform and Political Transition in Africa: The Quest for a Politics of Development." *World Politics* 49, no. 1 (1996): 92–129.

Lieberman, Evan S. "Taxation Data as Indicators of State-Society Relations: Possibilities and Pitfalls in Cross-National Research." *Studies in Comparative International Development* 36, no. 4 (2002): 89–115.

MacLean, Lauren Morris. "Solidarity in Crisis: Social Policies and Social Support Networks in Ghana and Côte d'Ivoire." Ph.D. diss., Department of Political Science, University of California at Berkeley, 2002.

Mamdani, Mahmood. *Citizen and Subject: Contemporary Africa and the Legacy of Late Colonialism.* Princeton: Princeton University Press, 1996.

Manning, Carrie L. "Democratic Transition in Mozambique, 1992–1995: Beginning at the End?" Ph.D. diss., Department of Political Science, University of California at Berkeley, 1997.

McMillan, Margaret, and William A. Masters. "A Political Economy Model of Agricultural Taxation, R&D and Growth in Africa." Discussion Paper 99-03, Department of Economics, Tufts University, January 1999.

Medani, Khalid. "Market Crocodiles in an Age of Cannibalism: The Role of the Parallel Market in State Formation and Collapse in Sudan and Somalia." M.A. thesis, Department of Political Science, University of California at Berkeley, 1995.

Médard, Jean-François. "The Underdeveloped State in Tropical Africa: Political Clientelism or Neo-Patrimonialism?" In *Private Patronage and Public Power: Political Clientelism in the Modern State,* edited by Christopher Clapham. New York: St. Martin's Press, 1982.

Melson, Robert, and Howard Wolpe. "Modernization and the Politics of Communalism: A Theoretical Perspective." *American Political Science Review* 64, no. 4 (1970): 1112–1130.

Migdal, Joel. *Strong Societies and Weak States: State-Society Relations and State Capabilities in the Third World.* Princeton: Princeton University Press, 1988.

Miller, Gary. "Confiscation, Credible Commitment, and Progressive Reform in the United States." *Journal of Institutional and Theoretical Economics* 145 (1989): 686–692.

Montgomery, John D. "Bureaucratic Politics in Southern Africa." *Public Administration Review* 46, no. 5 (1986).

———. "Probing Managerial Behavior: Image and Reality in Southern Africa." *World Development* 15, no. 7 (1987).

Mukandala, Rwekaza. *The Political Economy of Parastatal Enterprise in Tanzania and Botswana.* Ph.D. diss., Department of Political Science, University of California at Berkeley, 1988.

Ndulu, Benno, and Stephen O'Connell. "Governance and Growth in Sub-Saharan Africa." *Journal of Economic Perspectives* 13, no. 3 (1999): 41–66.

Ndulu, Benno, and Nicolas van de Walle, eds. *Agenda for Africa's Economic Renewal.* New Brunswick: Transaction Publishers, 1996.

Nellis, Nahalel. "Deficiencies in European Monetary Union's Credible Commitment Against Monetary Expansion." *Cornell International Law Journal* 33 (2000): 263–296.

North, Douglass. "Institutions and Credible Commitment." *Journal of Institutional and Theoretical Economics* 149 (1993): 11–23.

———. *Institutions, Institutional Change, and Economic Performance.* Cambridge: Cambridge University Press, 1990.

O'Brien, Donal Cruise. *Saints and Politicians: Essays in the Organization of a Senegalese Peasant Society.* London: Cambridge University Press, 1975.

O'Connell, Stephen, and Charles Soludo. "Aid Intensity in Africa." *World Development* 29, no. 9 (2001): 1527–1552.

Oliver, Roland, and J. D. Fage. *A Short History of Africa.* Baltimore: Penguin Books, 1966.

Parhad, Rita, and Scott Straus. "An Emerging Norm of Humanitarian Intervention? The Case of Genocide." Paper delivered at the annual meeting of the American Political Science Association, Washington, D.C., August 31–September 3, 2000.

Price, Robert. *Society and Bureaucracy in Contemporary Ghana.* Berkeley: University of California Press, 1975.

Przeworski, Adam, Michael E. Alvarez, José Antonio Cheibub, and Fernando Limongi. *Democracy and Development: Political Institutions and Well-Being in the World, 1950–1990.* New York: Cambridge University Press, 2000.

Reed, Michael C. "Gabon: A Neo-Colonial Enclave of Enduring French Interest." *Journal of Modern African Studies* 25, no. 2 (1987).

Reno, William. *Warlord Politics and African States.* Boulder: Lynne Rienner Publishers, 1998.

Richards, Paul. *Fighting for the Rain Forest: War, Youth and Resources in Sierra Leone.* Oxford and Portsmouth, N.H.: James Currey/Heinemann, 1996.

Roberts, Richard. *Warriors, Merchants, and Slaves.* Stanford: Stanford University Press, 1987.

Rodrik, Dani. "Development Strategies for the Next Century." Paper presented at the conference on "Developing Economies in the 21st Century," Institute for Developing Economies, Japan External Trade Organization, January 26–27, 2000, Chiba, Japan.

Roth, Guenther. "Personal Rulership, Patrimonialism, and Empire-Building in New States." *World Politics* 20, no. 2 (1968): 194–206.

Russell, Alec. *Big Men, Little People: The Leaders Who Defined Africa.* New York: New York University Press, 2000.

Russett, Bruce, and Harvey Staff. *World Politics.* 5th ed. New York: W. H. Freeman, 1996.

Sachs, J. D., and M. Werner. "Sources of Slow Growth in African Economies." *Journal of African Economies* 6, no. 3 (1997): 335–376.

Sandbrook, Richard, with Judith Barker. *The Politics of Africa's Economic Stagnation.* Cambridge: Cambridge University Press, 1985.

Sanger, David. "Clinton Warns U.N. of a New Age of Civil Wars." *New York Times,* September 17, 2000, p. A1.

Schaffer, Frederic. *Democracy in Translation: Understanding Politics in an Unfamiliar Culture.* Ithaca: Cornell University Press, 1998.

Schatz, Sayre. "Structural Adjustment in Africa: A Failing Grade So Far." *Journal of Modern African Studies* 32, no. 4 (1994): 679–693.

———. "The World Bank's Fundamental Misconception in Africa." *Journal of Modern African Studies* 34, no. 2 (1996): 239–248.

Selznick, Philip. *Leadership in Administration.* New York: Harper and Row, 1957.

Shepsle, Kenneth. "Discretion, Institutions, and the Problem of Government Commitment." In *Social Theory for a Changing Society*, edited by Pierre Bourdieu and James Coleman. Boulder: Westview Press, 1991.

Spanier, John. *Games Nations Play*. 8th ed. Washington, D.C.: Congressional Quarterly, 1993.

Suleiman, Ezra N. *Elites in French Society: The Politics of Survival*. Princeton: Princeton University Press, 1978.

———. *Politics, Power and Bureaucracy in France: The Administrative Elite*. Princeton: Princeton University Press, 1974.

Theobald, Robin. "Patrimonialism." *World Politics* 34, no. 4 (1982): 548–559.

Thornton, John. *Africa and Africans in the Making of the Atlantic World, 1400–1800*. 2nd ed. Cambridge: Cambridge University Press, 1998.

Tomich, Thomas, Peter Kilby, and Bruce Johnston. *Transforming Agrarian Economies*. Ithaca: Cornell University Press, 1995.

United Nations. "Report of the Panel of Experts Appointed Pursuant to UN Security Council 1306 (2000), Document S/2000/1195, December 20, 2000.

———. "Report on the Panel of Experts on the Illegal Exploitation of Natural Resources and Other Forms of Wealth of the Democratic Republic of the Congo." Document S/2001/357, April 2001.

Vaill, Peter B. "The Purposing of High-Performing Systems." In *Leadership and Organizational Culture: New Perspectives on Administrative Theory and Practice*, edited by Thomas J. Sergiovanni and John E. Corbally. Urbana: University of Illinois Press, 1984.

van de Walle, Nicolas. *African Economies and the Politics of Permanent Crisis, 1979–1999*. Cambridge: Cambridge University Press, 2001.

van de Walle, Nicolas, and Timothy Johnston. *Improving Aid to Africa*. Baltimore: Johns Hopkins University Press, 1996.

Watts, Michael, ed. *State, Oil, and Agriculture in Nigeria*. Berkeley: Institute of International Studies, University of California, 1987.

Weber, Eugen. *Peasants into Frenchmen: The Modernization of Rural France, 1870–1914*. London: Chatto and Windus, 1979.

Weber, Max. *Economy and Society*, edited by G. Roth and C. Wittich. Berkeley: University of California Press, 1978.

Weiss, Thomas G. "On the Brink of a New Era? Humanitarian Interventions, 1991–1994." In *Beyond Traditional Peacekeeping*, edited by Donald C. F. Daniel and Bradd C. Hayes. New York: St. Martin's Press, 1995.

White, Leonard. *The Jacksonians: A Study in Administrative History: 1829–1861*. New York: Macmillan, 1954.

Widner, Jennifer. *Building the Rule of Law*. New York: W. W. Norton, 2001.

Williamson, Oliver. *The Economic Institutions of Capitalism: Firms, Markets, and Relational Contracting*. New York: Free Press, 1985.

Wolfensohn, James D. "The Other Crisis." Address to the Board of Governors, World Bank, October 6, 1998.

World Bank. *Accelerated Development in Sub-Saharan Africa: An Agenda for Action.* Washington, D.C.: World Bank, 1981.

———. *Assessing Aid: What Works, What Doesn't, and Why.* Washington, D.C. : Oxford University Press, 1998.

———. *Can Africa Claim the 21st Century?* Washington, D.C.: World Bank, 2000.

———. Heavily Indebted Poor Countries website, http://www.worldbank. org/hipc/Grouping_Final.xls.

———. *World Development Report 1997: The State in a Changing World.* Washington, D.C.: World Bank, 1997.

———. *World Development Report 2000/2001.* New York: Oxford University Press, 2001.

Yates, Douglas A. *The Rentier State in Africa: Oil Rent Dependency and Neocolonialism in the Republic of Gabon.* Trenton: Africa World Press, 1996.

Young, Crawford. *The African Colonial State in Comparative Perspective.* New Haven: Yale University Press, 1994.

Young, Crawford, and Thomas Turner. *The Rise and Decline of the Zairian State.* Madison: University of Wisconsin Press, 1984.

Zartman, I. William, ed. *Collapsed States: The Disintegration and Restoration of Legitimate Authority.* Boulder: Lynne Rienner Publishers, 1995.

Index

About the Book

THIS THOUGHTFUL DISCUSSION PROBES THE INTERNATIONAL ROOTS OF Africa's civil conflicts and lackluster economies. Analyzing an unwitting system that creates a set of incentives inimical to development, the authors offer a new way of thinking about Africa's development dilemmas and the policy options for addressing them.

Weak states, aid dependence, crushing debt, and enclave economies, argue the authors, create disincentives for long-term economic growth and even peace. The nature of Africa's interaction with the international system often supports these negative features; thus, the remedy must come from a radical restructuring of that relationship. *Africa's Stalled Development* heeds that call by presenting specific and innovative prescriptions for change that are sure to stimulate a much-needed debate.

David K. Leonard is dean of international and area studies and professor of political science at the University of California at Berkeley. He has been working in and on Africa since 1963. **Scott Straus**, formerly a Nairobi-based journalist, is at present at the University of California at Berkeley, completing dissertation research on the Rwandan genocide.